Orkney 1993

To Audrew

from the

Shoal
and
Sheaf

The Orkney Library, established in 1683, is the oldest
public library in Scotland.
In 1909 the new library building in Kirkwall was opened by its
benefactor Dr Andrew Carnegie, the American industrialist.

Shoal and Sheaf

ORKNEY'S PICTORIAL HERITAGE

Selection and commentary
DAVID M.N. TINCH

Photographic reproduction
DAVID MACKIE

Introduction
GEORGE MACKAY BROWN

THE
BLACKSTAFF
PRESS

BELFAST

for Moyra

First published in 1988 by
The Blackstaff Press Limited
3 Galway Park, Dundonald, Belfast BT16 0AN, Northern Ireland
Reprinted 1989

© Photographs, The Orkney Library, 1988
© Introduction, George Mackay Brown, 1988
© Text, David M.N. Tinch, 1988
All rights reserved

Printed by Oxford University Press

British Library Cataloguing in Publication Data
Shoal and sheaf: Orkney's pictorial
heritage.
1. Scotland. Orkney, 1837–
I. Tinch, David M.N.
941.1'3208
ISBN 0-85640-411-X

CONTENTS

Our hands reach across light to shoal and sheaf.

from
An Orkney Tapestry
George Mackay Brown

PREFACE

The Orkney Library is the oldest public library in Scotland, the earliest accepted date for its conception being 1683, when William Baikie of Holland on the island of Stronsay bequeathed his entire collection of books to the people of Kirkwall, where it came to be known as the Publick Bibliotheck of Kirkwall. This library was housed variously in St Magnus Cathedral, the old Tolbooth and Kirkwall Town Hall, but at the beginning of this century, under the revision of the existing library stock, most of it was considered unsuitable and sold by public roup. It was purchased by the late Archdeacon James B. Craven, who in turn left it to Aberdeen University Library, where it remains almost intact. In 1909 a new building to house the expanding Kirkwall Free Library was opened by its benefactor Dr Andrew Carnegie, the American industrialist; it still serves as headquarters for what is now the regional library service for Orkney.

The Orkney Photographic Archive was founded in 1976 as part of the library service with Barbara Walls's priceless gift of over 6,000 negatives, mostly on glass, produced by the late Tom Kent. The collection has been expanded regularly since then with the acquisition of works by many other local photographers and it is now in excess of 16,000 negatives, dating from the 1860s to recent times. With the appointment of the professional photographer David Mackie in 1986, its full value is gradually being realised and though for a number of years the accent will necessarily be mainly concerned with conservation and indexing procedures, some limited use of the collection is now possible.

The archive is of immeasurable social and historical importance, both locally and nationally, since it records changes that were taking place throughout the country and events that were of interest nationwide. It depicts the change from horse-drawn transport to engine-powered vehicles; the introduction of the first air service to the islands; ships and shipwrecks; the gradual transition from traditional farming methods to the use of machines; the effects on Orkney of two world wars, including the great naval anchorage at Scapa Flow, the many visits of the British navy and the dramatic scuttling of the German High Seas Fleet in 1919; royal occasions; military parades; new buildings as well as what they replaced; important archaeological excavations; the restoration of St Magnus Cathedral; industries that have largely disappeared, like kelp-making, peat-cutting and the herring fishing industry; local crafts and customs; and people of interest. There are also many plates of great scenic and aesthetic value.

The quality of photography is in the main of a very high technical standard and many of the photographs have already been used in books, postcards and magazines. We are fortunate to have such an invaluable asset and for this we are indebted firstly to the skills and endeavours of our early photographers and secondly to those who had the good sense to collect and hold on to old prints and negatives and, in time, to pass them over to the Orkney Photographic Archive so that they may be of benefit to us all. The work of only a few is illustrated in this book – the selection being dependent upon content rather than choice of photographer.

There are many people who are due my grateful thanks for help given over the past year. It would be difficult to acknowledge them all and I hope that those not individually named will accept a general thank you, sincerely felt. I must, however, make special mention of the following: David Mackie, our photographic archivist, whose expertise has contributed largely to the success of this book; George Mackay Brown, who very kindly wrote the introduction; Anne Cormack, who took on the tedious but necessary task of proofreading the script; Michael Moss for his initial advice on producing a book of photographs; Tommy Tulloch, Bryce Wilson and Alison Fraser for supplying information; George Leonard for permission to use some of the Kent prints from his private collection; and last, but by no means least, Orkney Islands Council for backing the venture.

David M.N. Tinch
Kirkwall, Orkney, 1988

INTRODUCTION

IT IS HARD TO IMAGINE WHAT ORCADIANS thought of their ancestors, and of their history, before photography. It is possible that for the majority of people the belief was that life did not change much: the clothes people wore and the houses they lived in had been very much the same for centuries. They had rents to pay and a precarious living to win from land and sea. The rhythms of life in Kirkwall and Stromness were different from the rhythms of crofter–fishermen. There was a hierarchy of laird and government and queen. Wars broke out, and the Napoleonic Wars had touched them brutally: the press gang was part of their hoard of legend. But on the whole, they must have thought life was lived within a fixed frame; within it, extraordinary characters appeared from time to time: the tyrant Patrick Stewart and the pirate John Gow, and the sisterhood of witches that had been burned at Gallowsha in Kirkwall.

Instead of newspapers the people of Orkney had gossip that was spun from mouth to mouth at well and smithy. If the gossip was strange and well founded, it could harden into a story that might last for a few generations. If the story had a quality that touched some inner core of our human condition, it hardened into legend, and assumed qualities akin to poetry. Beyond the legend lies the myth, which is often too dense and rich for us to unravel. But myth, we might believe, contains the essence of what our remote ancestors experienced; and so those very primitive stories endured, passed on from generation to generation like heirlooms that belong to the whole community, and whose first makers are lost and anonymous. But if our Orcadian great-grandfathers, sitting at the smithy forge or in an alehouse, thought of the people of those legends and myths at all, they must have imagined them as rather like themselves, living between the hill and the shore, and wearing roughly the same clothes and speaking the same words. Only the magic, whether bright or dark, was lost.

With the coming of the scientific age, everything changed. There was a new kind of magic abroad. Time was not cyclical in its movement (who could have doubted it in former times, considering the cycle of the seasons, and the different cycles of sun and moon and stars; and of the lives of men). Now, for humankind at least, the sign of the age was linear, a straight sure progress – with interruptions and hold-ups and hitches now and then, to be sure – from savagery and poverty and superstition along a golden road of Progress and Prosperity.

It is difficult now to tell what a change of outlook this new materialistic creed wrought in a fairly simple community like Orkney. New inventions proliferated: steamships, reapers, clothes and ornaments brought from factories in the south. There was universal education; it was thought that the minds of ordinary people would be immeasurably widened and that the more intelligent pupils could thereby raise themselves out of the hardship and poverty that had been the immemorial lot of their ancestors.

Among the abundance of inventions was the camera, and this book is beholden entirely to photography. Now we can see plainly our ancestors' garb and gear and style of living; and we can see this period of our social history when Orkney, in common with the rest of the western world, was being caught up and thrown forward on a great wave of change.

No one can doubt that there have been vast improvements, in housing and health, in agriculture and trade and fishing. We live lives of leisure and plenty compared to the Orcadians of 1870. We have far more information and knowledge of the world around us. Many dreads and anxieties have been lightened, if not entirely lifted: our fishermen and farmers are not so utterly at the mercy of weather and the 'black worm'. Certainly, on the whole, for the average person, life in Orkney is much pleasanter now.

But perhaps there has been a price to pay. 'Where is the wisdom we have lost in knowledge?' asked T.S. Eliot and Gerard Manley Hopkins's plea has a special meaning today: 'Let them be left; wildness and wet. . .' Rarer and rarer in our over-cultivated fields are those lovely companions of our mortality, the birds and wildflowers and small creatures. There will never be such a time again as is so richly depicted in this book.

The old cyclical movement has, it seems, anyway, to have been cast aside. All is change and flux, and the wonders of science and technology. Those who look at photographs – or the equivalent – of us in, say, 2070 may be even more lost in wonderment: that is, if there are people in the world at all then (so perilous is our hold on the earth) or if technology has not robbed us of the faculty of wonder.

George Mackay Brown
December 1987
Stromness, Orkney

THE VAGARIES OF NATURE

Ir is not possible to live in orkney and not be aware of nature in all its forms. It influences, and indeed at times dominates, life here to a degree that incomers may find astonishing. The weather is not only a daily source of conversation, but a factor that has to be considered as we go about our everyday chores. A storm that would wreak havoc of disastrous proportions in the cosseted south is something that is accepted and expected here on a regular basis. Structures are rarely knocked down or blown away because we build accordingly. When we fall short of this standard and damage is done, we learn a lesson and replace it with something that will stand. Life goes on, work goes on, and if it is not possible to do anything outside, then we find something that needs doing inside, each day regulated to a familiar weather pattern.

At the other extreme, it is possible to wander over one of our many hills or along our empty shore on a day so still that the only sounds to be heard are the gentle rippling of water on a sandy beach or in a nearby burn, accompanied perfectly by a chorus of bird song. Long dark winter days, when the daylight barely breaks through, are amply compensated for in midsummer, when the sun hardly sets. Our weather is unpredictable, no two days are alike, and to live here one must accept that and enjoy it, whatever it offers.

The sea is another element that governs our lives. We are brought up with it. Its shores are our playground when we are young and where we relax when we grow up. It is a constant and familiar part of our environment; we depend upon it for bringing in what we need and exporting what we produce, and we take part of our living from it. It is generous in what it gives, but at times it can exact a heavy price. Like the weather, we rely upon it, we understand it to a degree, we respect it, but we ignore it at our peril.

We are also blessed with a wide range of wildlife. Flowers, birds and animals abound, including certain species that are unique to our islands. Nature reserves and bird sanctuaries are welcome here. We have lived in harmony with nature for centuries and though it has provided food for our table, fertiliser for our land, feathers for our pillows and oil for our lamps, it was never plundered as it has been in other parts of the world. We have been content to take what we need and have left it to balance its own books.

Eroded over the centuries by the continuous actions of fierce tides and heavy seas, Orkney has many spectacular rock formations around its coastline, particularly on its western ramparts. Here, the unpredictable waters of the Atlantic make their presence known sometimes with gentle caressing movements that can scarcely be heard above the cries of the sea birds, but at other times thundering in before storm-force winds, sending out shock waves that can be heard and felt a mile inland. Some are well known, like the Old Man of Hoy, a large pinnacle of rock that rears 450 feet out of the sea, attracting climbers from all over the world, or St John's Head, the highest sheer cliff in Britain, dropping vertically for 1,140 feet. Caves, rock stacks and 'geos', or ravines, abound and have not been missed over the years by the artistic eyes of our painters and photographers. This is a view of Scabra Head on the island of Rousay, taken from Sinian's Cave.

PHOTOGRAPH BY TOM KENT, *c.* 1920

On 24 September 1909 a thunderstorm of 'unparalleled severity' struck parts of Orkney. A local man, Peter Hendry, was killed by lightning while driving a bus on Scapa Road. After a cloudburst, a wall of water cascaded down the Papdale valley on the main island, through Mill Street, Queen Street, Bridge Street, Albert Street and Junction Road. It tore down walls and carried hen coops, sheds and other structures before it. One old woman, Mrs Cutt, had to be rescued from her home by neighbours, who had to break down the door with sledgehammers after water had poured through her window to a depth of 4½ feet. At the lower end of town extensive damage was done in shops, rendering useless groceries, drapery and other goods, and many houses were badly soiled inside. At the other end, water rushed down Clay Loan 'like a river' into Main Street and Victoria Street. Flooding in Kirkwall is not an unusual occurrence in certain low-lying parts of the town but it is normally as a result of exceptionally high tides rather than by rain water. In this view of Albert Street the residents, old and young, appear to be taking it all in their stride.

PHOTOGRAPH BY TOM KENT, 1909

5

Gales are an accepted part of life in Orkney, particularly during the months of January and February. On 15 November 1920, after a storm had raged for seven days and nights, considerable damage was recorded throughout the county. At Scapa, the pier was badly affected, huge blocks of stone, some as large as 6 feet by 4 feet by 20 inches, were dislodged and thrown about, one through the wall of the admiralty store. A shed was swept away and an iron crane was wrecked. On the approach road from the pier to the seaplane station, the sea wall was breached in three places, creating one 40-foot gap, almost removing the road at one point, and from the seaplane base westward, the wall was almost entirely destroyed. The seaplane slipway was smashed, and many sea birds and several sheep in a nearby field were killed. From the beach, a boat was lifted bodily into the air, landed on its stem, split and then blown a considerable distance inland, levelling a fence on its way. Yet curiously the expressions of these faces seem to imply that the taking of a photograph was more of a phenomenon than the storm.

PHOTOGRAPHS BY TOM KENT, 1920

Wild blue lupins grew in abundance in certain parts of Orkney, particularly in the parishes of Harray and Sandwick on the main island, giving a spectacular display around mid-June. It is believed that they were introduced here about 1860 by William Traill of Westness on the island of Rousay, apparently to enrich poor-quality or gravelly heath with nitrogen to make it more suitable for cultivation. Some specimens were sent to Kew and aroused great interest since they were not indigenous to Britain. However, modern cultivation methods have all but removed them, apart from a few odd corners where they have escaped and survived. This little girl from Harray almost looks in danger of getting lost among lupins, some as tall as herself.

PHOTOGRAPH BY TOM KENT, 1930

THE GOLDEN WEST. ORKNEY.

Orkney winters are long, stormy and very dark. Some compensation for this comes from the long summer evenings, particularly in June when the sun never really sets. Dawn follows dusk immediately and it is a long-standing custom here to play midnight golf or midnight bowls in midsummer. Sunsets are among the most spectacular to be found anywhere and Tom Kent rarely missed an opportunity to capture one in all its glory. The fact that his prints are in black and white hardly detracts from the effect.

PHOTOGRAPH BY TOM KENT, *c.* 1920

SCENIC ORKNEY

ALMOST ANY PICTURE IN THIS BOOK WOULD QUALIFY for this chapter but for convenience it has been focused on traditional landscape photographs which were taken primarily for their aesthetic qualities. There have been changes since these scenes were photographed but the essence remains and they may tempt new visitors to our lovely islands. They may also help to remind Orcadians of the beauty that surrounds us which we daily take for granted.

An attractive view over the western approach to
Scapa Flow, with the hills of the island of Hoy
shrouded in mist. Taken on the main island from
the Brae of Wit, called after the farm in the
picture, which leads down to the kirkyard at
Warbeth. The cluster of buildings shown here
nearest Hoy, is the Farm of Wit, since renovated;
the building on its right has now gone. Together
with the building in the foreground, they
illustrate a variety of roofing techniques in vogue
at the time.

PHOTOGRAPH BY TOM KENT, *c.* 1900

A tranquil scene in the village of Finstown on the main island, the home of photographers William Hugh Wood and Tom Kent, and situated about midway between the two main towns of Kirkwall and Stromness. This picture was taken from just outside the village smithy, now known as Smithy Cottage. Two of the cottages have been upgraded to two-storey houses, garden dykes have been built and kerbs have been installed; otherwise this view has changed little. The village is now a popular residential area for commuters, working mainly in Kirkwall.

PHOTOGRAPH BY TOM KENT, *c.* 1900

A peaceful setting at the Barony in the main-island village of Birsay, which has not changed in essence since this photograph was taken: buildings have been restored or improved, rather than replaced. The Earl's Palace, the remains of which stand in the background, is a constant reminder of an era that was far from peaceful. Founded in 1574 by the tyrannous Robert Stewart, Earl of Orkney, and completed by his equally infamous son Patrick, its ominous presence loomed over this tiny hamlet for many years as father and son wreaked havoc among the crofters of Orkney, before being arrested, tried and executed in Edinburgh in 1615. Another important historical site, the famous Viking settlement on the Brough of Birsay, lies just offshore from the village. The burn in the foreground is the water source which still drives the only working grain mill in Orkney, at Boardhouse, about a mile upstream.

PHOTOGRAPH BY TOM KENT, *c.* 1900

A panoramic view of St Margaret's Hope on the island of South Ronaldsay, taken from the east. The village consists of two main streets, simply named Back Road and Front Road. Like Stromness on the main island, many of its houses sit directly over the sea, with private slipways, many of which were destroyed by the gales of the early 1950s. Formerly known as Rognvaldsvoe, there was a popular belief that it was renamed in memory of Margaret, Maid of Norway and legal heiress to the Scottish throne, who died in Orkney in 1290 on her way to marry Edward, son of Edward I of England. It was, in fact, named after a small chapel in the area dedicated to St Margaret. The village was an important fishing station for a time, still evident when this photograph was taken by the number of fishing boats in use and the roof of the nearest building which was the herring curing station. The building on the shore, partly constructed from old boats, was William Petrie's boatyard. The village is now accessible from the main island via the Churchill Barriers, built by Italian prisoners of war during the Second World War to protect the naval anchorage at Scapa Flow.

PHOTOGRAPH BY GEORGE W. WILSON, *c.* 1890

Another of Orkney's villages which grew up around the herring fishing industry, St Mary's in the main-island parish of Holm, still has many relics of those busy days. On the right is the old cooperage, with steps on the gable end, where barrels were assembled for the packers. The large boat is a fifie and the two in the foreground are Orkney yoles.

PHOTOGRAPH BY TOM KENT, *c.* 1920

A beautiful view over Houton in Orphir on the
main island at harvest time, looking towards the
island of Hoy. The jetty on the left was used
during the First World War for the seaplane
station and is now the main landing point for
commuters to the oil terminal on the island
of Flotta.

PHOTOGRAPH BY TOM KENT, *c.* 1900

An excellent panoramic view of the district of Rackwick on the island of Hoy. This picturesque spot had a thriving community at the time this photograph was taken, based on the traditional industries of crofting and of fishing, a hazardous occupation in the notorious waters of the Pentland Firth. When the fishing died the community died with it and for a time Rackwick was all but deserted. Houses were left derelict, many with their contents intact, giving the impression that perhaps some day the inhabitants would return. They never did. In recent years, however, the combination of a programme of rehabilitation, organised by the Hoy Trust, and its growing popularity as a place to have a holiday retreat has brought life back into the area. Among those who value its peace and tranquillity as a necessary tonic in our present materialistic and tormented world is the well-known composer Sir Peter Maxwell Davies.

PHOTOGRAPH BY GEORGE W. WILSON, *c.* 1890

A pleasant rural scene at Broughton on the island of Westray, showing an elderly woman plucking a hen. The houses are typical of the time with lime-built stone walls, heavy flagstone roof, the wooden structure at the front well protected by layers of tar, and the whole surrounded by a dry-stone dyke.

PHOTOGRAPH BY WILLIAM HOURSTON, *c.* 1930

THE NATIVES

WHAT IS AN ORCADIAN? This question has been considered many times but the most comprehensive study on this theme appeared in a recent book, *The People of Orkney*, edited by R.J. Berry and H.N. Firth. Contributions from experts on a whole range of subjects are included, covering archaeology, history, anthropology, genetics, and even a detailed investigation of our inherent blood groups. It is too wide a discussion to summarise here but it is clear that, like other races throughout the world, Orcadians have an identity that is very much their own. History shows that early invaders, such as the Picts, found a society already established; when the Vikings settled here they enforced their culture on the community, extending the ethnic mix once again; and later, as the feudal Scottish landowners were encouraged to impose their will upon the residents, further changes in our blood lines and social structure evolved.

What are the characteristics of the Orcadian? We are basically survivors. In spite of centuries of abuse by foreign raiders, governments and lairds, in spite of having to exist and thrive on an economy based on agriculture in a climate that is far from conducive to it, we are still here. Bullied, moulded, perhaps even coaxed into being what we are, we have stood the test of time, bent but not broken. Recognised for the warmth of our welcome, yet understandably wary of incomers; inclined to be a bit of a plodder, patient, dogged, not easy to provoke, slow to react, Orcadians are complex characters. As demonstrated by the exploits of William Balfour Baikie, explorer of the River Niger, of Dr John Rae and the thousands of Orcadians who carried the torch for the Hudson's Bay Company in northern Canada, and of the many Orcadians who have emigrated and prospered overseas, there is also resilience, determination, a sense of adventure when the opportunity presents itself and a degree of adaptability and innovation to see it through. And from our community, that by necessity is practical by nature, there has emerged a remarkable number of men and women who have distinguished themselves in the fields of art and science.

As Berry and Firth discovered, the more you try to analyse, the deeper you try to dig, the less sure you are of what you have found. An Orcadian is an Orcadian.

THE LOCH SIDE, BIRSAY, ORKNEY

A group of schoolchildren on the way home from school in Birsay on the main island. Though it illustrates a typical mix of ages, to be found in most one- or two-teacher schools, in this particular group the girls appear to be very much in the minority. Everyone is dressed in 'school best', with caps an essential part of the boys' attire.

Water has always held a great fascination for Orkney children, be it fresh or salt, still or running. Swimming was almost entirely confined to the sea, cold though it was, and along the beaches there were crabs to be caught, shells to be collected, sea birds and their eggs to be investigated, and treasures of all sorts to be found. Toy and model boats were constructed from all kinds of material – wood, paper, feathers or reeds. Rafts were built from driftwood, wooden barrels or washtubs and launched with great excitement. Boys were introduced to the real world of boats and fishing at an early age, many to make their living from the rich seas around our shores. Throwing stones, using different techniques to form a 'dead man's plunge' (breaking the water with no splash) or a 'skithery' or skimmer, caused many an aching arm. There were 'brandies' or sticklebacks to be caught, dams to be built, model water mills to construct, and a whole range of other activities invented by active young minds. Life was never dull when there was water at hand.

PHOTOGRAPH BY TOM KENT, c. 1920

The hurdy-gurdy man was a popular summer visitor around the turn of the century. He was one of several street entertainers, like the one-man band and the blind fiddler, who came to Orkney, particularly during the market time. Here he is complete with organ and monkey, in Dundas Street, Stromness, where he has attracted a varied audience. Most of the children seem to be well dressed and well shod but one small, bare-footed urchin stands apart from the rest. Chatting on the steps are two 'tinker' women wearing their distinctive shawls.

PHOTOGRAPH BY ROBERT H. ROBERTSON, c. 1900

Children fascinated Tom Kent and appear in
many of his photographs. Here is Sheriff William
Harvey's family at Berstane House outside
Kirkwall, during the period 1905–12 in which he
was Sheriff-substitute for Orkney. It makes a
striking contrast with Kent's study of the 'tinker'
children (opposite).

PHOTOGRAPH BY TOM KENT, c. 1909

Three 'tinker' children on their way
home from the beach with a collection
of firewood and other spoils. The
evident hand-me-down clothes were
the common lot of all poorer children
of the time but here they appear to
have been handed down more often
than most. The mixture of expressions
on their faces tends to reflect their
allotted place in society.

PHOTOGRAPH BY TOM KENT, *c*. 1900

23

Over the years Orkney, as elsewhere, has had its share of travelling people, known variously as pedlars, gypsies, or more commonly here as 'tinkers'. They moved around from place to place in a pony and trap or on foot, usually sleeping in tents or outhouses. They fulfilled a useful function doing all sorts of odd jobs, harvest work, making and mending, or peddling household items like pots or crockery. Owing to the inclement weather in Orkney, fires were usually installed inside the tent, with a chimney protruding through a hole in the roof. Though most have gone now, some eventually settled here, only to lose their identity as they gradually allowed their lives to be integrated into the normal life of the community.

This family has set up 'houses' near the old slaughterhouse in Stromness. The tent stands end on and looks smaller than it would have been. Nevertheless, it would seem that some additional accommodation would have been necessary. The pony and trap was common to these families. The basket of crockery, and further dishes inside the tent, are ready for the day's business. The old boathouse or shed in the background was another common feature of Orkney life in bygone years.

PHOTOGRAPH BY ROBERT H. ROBERTSON, *c.* 1900

Before the affluence of today, when parents tend to shower their children with expensive and often unwanted games and toys of all kinds, youngsters had to make their own amusement. Orkney was no exception to this and the convenience of plenty of water and a safe environment in which to run freely offered plenty of scope. Here is a group of boys at the Willow Burn in Kirkwall still in their school or Sunday 'best', totally immersed in what they are doing, and enjoying themselves with paper boats. Inevitably it would have led to wet feet, muddy clothes and a 'skelped erse', but this was accepted as part and parcel of a day's enjoyment. Clothes would be washed, feet and eyes would be dried and the whole process would probably happen all over again the following day.

PHOTOGRAPH BY TOM KENT, *c.* 1900

These young lads, at the Corn Slip in Kirkwall Harbour, are indulging in one of their popular pastimes – catching crabs. All that was required was a piece of cord or thread and bait. Unlike fishing, the bait was not dropped at random into unseen depths but laid precisely and invitingly between the claws of the unsuspecting crab. When it grabbed the bait, any hope of success depended on pulling it, quickly but gently, from the sea bed on to dry land before it realised what was happening. Once landed, it was dropped into a bucket or large tin full of salt water, the object being to see who caught the most and the biggest. At the end of the day several containers of wiser, but not much older, crabs would have been tipped back into the sea and, oblivious to the fact that they reeked strongly of fish, this happy, hungry bunch of lads would have made their way home.

PHOTOGRAPH BY DAVID HORNE, c. 1900

Lobster fishing has been a valuable commercial enterprise in Orkney for many years. It ranges from the man with a small boat and a few creels or lobster pots, catching mainly for his own use, to the large custom-built boats, carrying many creels and fishing on a purely business footing. Most of what used to be caught was sent to London, but now the markets are much wider – mainly Paris, Hamburg, Amsterdam, Bergen and other European cities – and the local industry is mainly controlled by three exporters. By 1834 around 100,000 lobsters were shipped annually and current production remains about the same. Creels are constructed of hooped iron and string netting, with a gate to allow the lobster in, tempted by bait, which then closes to bar any escape. A stone is attached to weigh the creel down to the sea bed and a rope is attached to floats or buoys to enable them to be pulled up when required. When caught, lobsters are preserved in wooden boxes in the sea, or more recently in the specially constructed lobster ponds in Kirkwall or Stromness, until ready for transporting. It is imperative that they are kept alive until they are to be cooked.

This lobster fisher from Birsay on the main island is loaded with freshly made ropes and floats for his creels, which would have been stacked somewhere along the beach beside his boat.

PHOTOGRAPH BY TOM KENT, c. 1900

27

Town sanitation became part of the public health effort to combat disease. An important person in this campaign was the local 'scaffie' or street-sweeper, who plied his trade through the streets of Kirkwall, pushing his heavy barrow over cobbles, tidying up the town with his heather 'besom'. This sweeper may have been William Borwick, who, with his son Robert, kept the streets of Kirkwall clean for many years.

PHOTOGRAPH BY TOM KENT, *c.* 1910

Annie Harper lived in a small one-chimneyed cottage called Quarryholes in the main-island parish of Rendall. Like many eccentrics, she was credited with having occult powers and sometimes referred to as a country 'spae-wife' or fortune-teller. She lived on a few shillings per week from the local Parochial Board and yet, when she died, she left the princely sum of £10, which must have been saved penny by penny over many years. She had several dogs, often carried in the straw 'cubbie' that was always on her back. They were known variously as Bozo Tom, Bozo Ann, Bessie Campbell after the local minister's wife, and General Burroughs in honour of the notorious landowner from the island of Rousay. She visited regularly in the area where she lived and many a small gift was slipped into her straw cubbie by a kindly neighbour. Her clothing defied description—layer upon layer piled on top of each other and tied at various points with coarse string. She lived to a good old age, latterly tended to by a caring neighbour, and when she died, she left no known relatives.

PHOTOGRAPH BY TOM KENT, *c.* 1900

The gentleman mounting a penny-farthing bicycle was an eccentric known locally as 'Skatehorn'. His real name was William Laughton and it is believed that he was born in Kincardine O'Neil, Aberdeenshire, his father being from Glasgow and his mother from Ireland. Though he came here as a pedlar, it is known that he served in the Naval Coast Volunteers, where he learned the arts of boxing and fencing. He also had a certain reputation for his ability to play the one-stringed fiddle. Though he lived for a time in Burger's Bay, Kirkwall, he spent most of his life on the road, preferring to sleep rough if the weather was good or in a barn or outhouse if it was not. It is said that when ill he lay like an animal until he recovered, often with no shelter other than a 'faely dyke'. He visited many farms and houses where he was not unkindly treated, often eating with the families. Many stories have been told of Skatehorn, some humorous, many true, others probably made up. He eventually died in the local county home. It appears that he was a particular favourite of Tom Kent, who took many photographs of him, often skilfully transferring his image from one print to another.

PHOTOGRAPH BY TOM KENT, c. 1900

30

The subject of this early portrait has obviously returned from the Nor'west where, during a spell with the fur-trading Hudson's Bay Company, he has acquired a jacket made of animal skin and decorated by Indians. The Hudson's Bay Company was established in 1670 and by 1704 records show that Orcadians were already in its employment. By the 1790s Orcadians provided about three-quarters of its manual work force in Canada, their qualities of endurance, self-reliance, doggedness and physical strength being particularly suitable for the rigours of life at the 'Bay'. An agent was appointed in Stromness to recruit labour and the company's ships called regularly to pick up fresh blood and to bring others back home. But many never saw their native land again, falling victim to attacks by Indians, the rival French, wild animals, or to the ravages of frostbite, disease, exhaustion and starvation. Others made fame and fortune and settled there, their descendants still to be found throughout the area. For a few it was a constant conflict of interests with a wife and family in Orkney, and another home with a 'squaw' or Indian wife and children in Canada. Even now, it is not unusual to find a Canadian of obvious Indian descent with the surname Drever, Flett, or Louttit. Some came home disillusioned and took up the life of a crofter or fisherman again and as the herring fishing industry developed in Orkney during the early years of the nineteenth century so the financial attraction of the 'Bay' grew less. But as in all communities there were always a few who wanted to break the shackles and seek their fortune elsewhere and this spirit ensured the continuation of the Hudson's Bay Company's interest in Orkney for many years.

PHOTOGRAPH BY WILLIAM H. WOOD, c. 1870

Two typical, sturdy young Orcadians, descended from men and women formed by generations of constant toil and hardship. Their dress, from the very substantial boots to the decorative hats, has clearly been given a lot of thought, blending practical necessity with the desire to be well presented. The children would have had little or no say in the choice and this, combined with a distinct distrust of the appliance confronting them, is clearly defined in their expressions.

PHOTOGRAPH BY WILLIAM H. WOOD, *c.* 1870

FOLLOWING THE HERRING

FISHING HAS ALWAYS PLAYED AN IMPORTANT PART in Orkney's economy. The old adage that an Orcadian was a farmer with a boat, but a Shetlander was a fisherman with a croft, reflects the fact that Orkney has always had agriculture as its main industry, while Shetland has leaned predominantly on fishing – that is until the influx of oil. However, there was a period at the end of the nineteenth century and the beginning of the twentieth when herring fishing threatened, particularly in some areas, to oust farming as the major industry in Orkney.

Built on a long tradition of taking a part-living from the sea, every island and parish had its fleet of yoles and skiffs, and in many areas, particularly on the islands of Stronsay, Burray and South Ronaldsay, organised curing, packing and marketing were well established long before the boom in the British fishing industry took place. In 1838 about 750 boats, mainly local, were fishing out of Orkney, employing some 3,340 men and boys, and about 1,800 coopers, curers, packers and other ancillary workers. Though the fishing was predominantly for herring, cod and ling were also important. The sudden boom in the industry exposed weaknesses in our traditional boats, including the Shetland sixareen, which had become part of the Orkney fishing scene. Even though the boats were built bigger, they could not compete with the faster and more seaworthy fifies, scaffies and, eventually, zulus, which were now following the herring in their seasonal move around the coasts of Britain, and it was these boats that became the backbone of the Orkney fishing fleet.

By 1898 Stromness had evolved as the major fishing port in Orkney, with thirty-eight stations scattered along its foreshore, from Ness to the North End. In 1901 it boasted a record catch of 43,594 crans, no mean brag when compared to the all-time record catch of 154,605 crans in 1912 for the whole of Orkney. With a normal resident population of under 2,000, it swelled to three times that number during the season, with some 2,000 fishermen and as many gutters, curers and packers. The boats, over 300 at one stage, came from Caithness, Sutherland, the east and north-east coasts of Scotland. The ancillary workers came from the same areas, plus a large contingent of women packers and gutters from the Western Isles. By 1908 the whole focus of the industry had transferred to the island of Stronsay, where it was to remain until 1939, by which time it had lost much of its aesthetic appeal, with the introduction of mass curing and of course the steam drifter.

The scenes in Stromness, or in Whitehall village on Stronsay, in those early days at the peak of a busy season must have been something to witness. Alive with the movement of hundreds of boats daily; carts, barrows and people all bustling about the harbour area; the whole cacophony of sound created by vehicles, barrels, boxes, hammers; the chants of the dealers; the chatter and songs of the workers – all concentrated in a limited area. Nothing like it exists in Orkney any more.

The Stromness herring fleet returning to harbour.
It was often claimed that you could walk from
one end of the town to the other on boats and on
this evidence it is not hard to believe. The earliest
boats to come to Orkney were fifies and scaffies.
The fifie's bow and stern were straight, while the
scaffies were raked. They were built from 25 feet
to 60 feet in length. The best features of both were
incorporated later in the zulu with a straight bow
and a raked stern, and they increased in size up to
80 feet.

PHOTOGRAPH BY TOM KENT, 1906

Some of the Stromness fishing fleet, hailing
mostly from Wick on mainland Scotland, as seen
from the South Pier. Gutters are working in front
of the building marked 'Fresh Fish' on Mowat
and Hay's Quay, which has now been extended
to become the new navigation school.

PHOTOGRAPH BY GEORGE W. WILSON, *c.* 1890

The fishing station at Ness in Stromness, belonging to Frederick William Stanger, played a prominent part in the industry at the beginning of this century. Though his business had been mainly shipbuilding – his boat-yard can be seen on the right, now the grounds of Stenigar where the Orkney artist Stanley Cursiter once lived – Stanger saw the opportunity to expand as the industry boomed. He squared off the shore with stone sea walls and built wooden jetties. He also constructed a number of small huts for the use of the fish-curers. Hundreds of barrels are lying in wait to be shipped to markets in the south or abroad to Germany or Russia. This site still has a boat-builder's yard but it is now mainly used by campers.

PHOTOGRAPH BY TOM KENT, *c.* 1900

These are the bent backs of the fisher girls down Clouston's Pier in Stromness. Their life was a hard one, moving from station to station as they followed the herring's seasonal migration, travelling mainly on the fishing boats themselves, often on rough seas, and carrying with them a trunk which contained their meagre possessions. The work was physically very demanding – herring perished quickly and markets had to be caught. It was rough on hands: the constant wetness, the coarse salt used for packing, and sharp knives all took their toll on cold numbed fingers. For protection rough bandages of hessian or other coarse material were applied. But they were a hardy lot, at most times happy and cheerful, and their banter and singing were a great feature of the fishing station. They came from both the east and west coasts of Scotland, particularly the Western Isles, often speaking only in Gaelic. Usually there were two gutters to one packer and, around 1900, they shared the rate of 3d. per barrel between them, with occasional bonuses. Coopers were also in attendance to seal the barrels. The herring was slit, gutted, graded and then rolled in salt before packing. The salt-water pump, in the foreground, would have been in constant use for cleaning purposes. The boats are clearly marked as hailing from Wick, Banff and Kirkcaldy on mainland Scotland.

PHOTOGRAPH BY TOM KENT, c. 1900

Fisher girls at their hut near Stromness. These huts, built for temporary accommodation, were home to these women wherever they travelled and were constructed simply of wood, felt and tar. They were basic but adequate, though clearly a serious fire hazard. However, they were a source of great pride to the women who stayed in them and who kept them immaculately clean, even to the point of whitewashing the floor under the polished iron stove. A copy of the workshop's rules and regulations was on display for their benefit. Personal possessions such as the melodion, Bibles, the lamps and letter racks would have been packed with their clothes in a trunk when they moved on. These photographs would have been taken on a Sunday since they are not at work, something that the strong religious element among them would never have conceded to.

PHOTOGRAPHS BY ROBERT H. ROBERTSON, c. 1900

Kirkwall too had its fishing fleet which almost
filled the Basin at peak times. The photograph
opposite captures the picturesque scenes that
were created by the departure and arrival of the
herring boats at dawn or dusk.

PHOTOGRAPHS BY TOM KENT, *c.* 1900

40

The treatment of larger fish, such as cod or halibut, was more complicated than that of herring. The fish were gutted, beheaded, then split and half the backbone, next to the head, was removed. Then they were washed, usually in sea water, to remove any particles of blood or guts and placed skin side up in a vat, between layers of salt. After some days they were taken out, washed and brushed off, drained of water, and spread out on the ground to dry in the sun. They were then built into a large stack or 'steeple', which was rebuilt in reverse order to keep the pressure even. This took place between mid-June and September. When ready, they were tied into bundles and stored, before being shipped to markets in the south. Heads, roes, livers and so on were taken home by employees for food. This photograph shows the gutting and cleaning process at Thomas Chalmers's fish store on the Ayre Road, Kirkwall, which is now a bus depot.

The water pump and salt vat can be seen in the background.

The photograph opposite shows the drying area at the Peedie Sea, behind the Ayre Mills, with fish being stacked into a steeple.

PHOTOGRAPHS: ABOVE BY GEORGE W. WILSON, *c.* 1890; OPPOSITE BY TOM KENT, *c.* 1900

An interesting study of a fisherman baiting his line. This was a time-consuming process, with many hooks to fill, usually with limpets or mussels, and great care had to be exercised in stowing the line in its box to avoid entanglement as it was fed over the stern. Lines like these, with hooks suspended a few feet below the surface, were either pulled behind the boat across the tide or set for a time in a fixed position, with buoys to keep the hooks from fouling the sea bed. The latter practice was more suitable for the crofter or smallholder whose main living came from working the land. For him it was an additional source of income, as well as a means of feeding his family. There was plenty of scope for this type of fishing in Orkney, with the vast number of tidal streams running between the islands, and a great variety of fish was caught in this way. On a good day halibut, cod, ling, skate, haddock, saithe, mackerel and other attractive species were hauled aboard but sometimes a whole day's fishing could be bedevilled by a shoal of dogfish or eels. This man's working facilities, from the soup plate of bait in his lap to the creel or lobster pot standing on end as a bench, were clearly an arrangement that had been tried and tested over many years.

PHOTOGRAPH BY DAVID HORNE, *c.* 1900

Whitehall village on the island of Stronsay was the hub of the herring fishing industry in Orkney for many years. The original house and estate of Whitehall, named by Patrick Fea in the seventeenth century, evolved slowly as a village, initially around the kelp trade, introduced by James Fea in 1722, but blossomed into its present size during the nineteenth century, when it became recognised as one of Scotland's major fishing ports. The pier and the village were constructed in the early 1800s by Malcolm Laing of Papdale, outside Kirkwall, specifically for fishermen, curers, gutters, coopers and shopkeepers. By 1840 it was prospering well, with about 400 local boats sailing out of it. The second half of the nineteenth century and the beginning of the twentieth saw a takeover by boats from outside, particularly from the east coast of Scotland, and the harbour expanded rapidly.

Each season the village erupted with excitement and colour as the herring boats arrived, and it seemed as if things would never change. But change they did: the days of the sailing boats were numbered as steam drifters gradually took over in the early 1900s. By 1913 there were 300 drifters based at Whitehall with 2,400 fishermen and 1,500 support workers, and there were 28 curing stations along its seafront. After a lull during the First World War years, it recovered once more and by 1924, the peak of the drifter era, 250,000 hundredweight of fish were exported, fetching over £100,000. The boom continued during the early 1930s but the effects of a general slump in the industry began to take its toll and by 1937 it was all over. Any attempts to revive it were killed off by the Second World War, and Whitehall was no longer a fishing port.

Here is the village in healthier times; on the right stands the fish mart, a hive of activity every Tuesday morning at the peak of the season in July and August, with auctioneers, dealers, clerks, fishermen, curers, and barrow boys all bustling about. By autumn each year the activity had gone. The boats with their crews and the whole entourage of ancillary workers had moved south to follow the migrating herring, the 'oncas' or casual workers had returned to their farms, the houses were empty, the mart closed, the pier deserted, and Whitehall village 'died' for another year.

PHOTOGRAPH BY TOM KENT, *c.* 1910

A LIVING FROM THE LAND

Taking a living out of the land still has its problems, but a hundred, even fifty, years ago, it was a precarious and often hopeless existence. 'Lady Luck' played a dominating role in the fortunes of the Orkney farmer. The quality of the soil, the size of the 'place', the health of the crofter and his family and his livestock, the attitude of the laird, and above all – the joker of the pack – the weather, all exerted their influence in the hand she dealt. It was never a fat living, unless you were one of the exalted few who owned a large estate on the islands, but it did vary greatly from the comparative comfort of a manager in the home farm of one of the more enlightened lairds, down to the despairing poverty of the smallholder who faced times when nothing was going for him. Neither the hardship, nor the good times, of the farming community were lost on our early photographers.

Mixed farming was the normal practice in Orkney up until the end of the Second World War, with each farm or croft rearing a variety of livestock, including cattle, pigs, sheep and poultry and, of course, horses for work. Before the days of 'battery' hens and the intensive feeding of turkeys and geese for the Christmas table, all poultry were free range. They were reared mainly for home consumption or to provide eggs for small local shops and both poultry and eggs had a great deal more flavour, particularly those that came from places near the seashore, than is normal today. From incubation to old age the fowl were carefully tended, usually by the farmer's wife, and they became so familiar to her that many came to be known individually by name. When the day came that one had to be 'put down' it was not altogether a happy occasion, particularly if Jessie or Teenie had become a particular favourite with one of the children. Its neck was discreetly 'thrawn', then it was plucked, cleaned and stuffed with oatmeal, all done out of sight to save unnecessary grief. Nothing was wasted – the meat was boiled or roasted, the neb and feet skinned to make soup, the giblets used to make gravy and the feathers used for pillows or cushions.

PHOTOGRAPH BY TOM KENT, *c.* 1900

47

Little hand-milking will be found in Orkney today, apart from the occasional house with an acre to spare where a cow or two is kept simply to provide milk for the family, or where there is an animal of a particularly obstinate nature which will not be milked in any other way. Fifty years ago all dairy cattle were hand-milked and on a large farm this occupied a number of people, both men and women, for a considerable time each day. It was usually done twice a day, though three milkings were not uncommon, and this was only the beginning of a number of chores, ranging from giving the cats and young calves their ration, up to the more complicated procedures of cooling and separating the cream from the skimmed milk, prior to making butter or cheese, and finally, of course, the meticulous cleaning-up process. Apart from cheese and butter another popular by-product was the residue from butter-making, simply known as buttermilk or by its local name 'blatho'. It was drunk in great quantities and had a sharp tangy taste that quenched the thirst as well as offering nourishment. It was also used extensively in baking.

The continuous finger-and-hand exercise involved in milking over many years built up exceptional hand strength, even in women, and the tale is still told of one particular old woman who could crush an apple in either hand with little effort.

PHOTOGRAPH BY DAVID HORNE, *c.* 1900

The farming year began in February with the cold, wearisome occupation of 'following the plough', a chore which initiated a chain of events that eventually led to harvest. Rarely begun before Candlemas (2 February) – the day that was considered to be the deadline – ploughing began as soon after as weather conditions allowed. Ploughmen often put in two four-hour yokes per day, the acreage covered depending upon the nature and condition of the soil, the type of plough and whether it was pulled by ox or horse. It was a long, hard day at the best of times and when it finished, it was accepted that the horses or oxen had to be watered, housed and fed before the ploughman could expect any food or rest.

This plough was the type commonly in use at the end of the nineteenth century, with a light iron frame, usually made by the local blacksmith. Earlier ploughs had been constructed of wood with an iron 'sock' or ploughshare. It was clearly not unusual for women to help out with this heavy chore.

PHOTOGRAPH BY GEORGE W. WILSON, c. 1890

To continue the clod-breaking process, harrows were used to grind the earth down even more. They have taken various forms over the years. At first, sturdy wooden frames were constructed, with fixed, rigid teeth of wood or iron projecting downwards into the soil. They were initially made small, designed to be pulled by a man or sometimes a woman, but as the ox or horse were employed to supply the power, they became much larger, often with an iron frame. To overcome the problem of breaking teeth, curved spring-toothed harrows became fashionable and they continued well after the arrival of mechanical traction.

PHOTOGRAPH BY TOM KENT, *c.* 1900

After ploughing, several processes were needed to break the soil down into a finer tilth for sowing crops. Clod-breaking and harrowing were the principal methods, though some rolling was also practised. Clod breaking involved many hours of hacking with 'eatches', a form of heavy hoe or adze designed for the purpose, or, alternatively, as seen here, by dragging a heavy flagstone over the rough ground, with the driver standing on it for additional weight.

PHOTOGRAPH BY TOM KENT, *c.* 1900

Turnips are believed to have been known in Orkney by the end of the seventeenth century, some time before potatoes arrived. Introduced as a garden crop, they remained so for many years but by the early nineteenth century there were indications that they were developing into a field crop, when it was recorded that they were being cultivated in drills on the island of Burray. Gradually, as their value as food for animals as well as humans was recognised, the area of land allocated for 'neeps' on each farm grew and they became established as part of the crop-rotation sequence. Earlier attempts at broadcasting the seeds proved to be impractical as there was some difficulty in keeping the area clear of weeds. The well-tilled and manured soil was therefore ploughed into drills, 27–30 inches apart, and the seeds sown. As the leaves appeared, the turnips had to be 'singled', a process that reduced their numbers to one every 8–10 inches along the drills. This was achieved by pushing out the excess plants with a hoe, designed for the purpose. This is a team of 'singlers' at the farm of Papdale, near Kirkwall, each with his or her own drill, and working in unison from left to right.

PHOTOGRAPH BY TOM KENT, *c.* 1900

Potatoes were introduced to Orkney during the early part of the eighteenth century to supplement the traditional crops of bere and oats and they became particularly popular in areas where fish, cabbage and kail was the staple diet. Like turnips, they arrived as a garden crop but were soon expanded into a full field crop, fitting into the normal sequence of crop rotation. Though some preferred the simple method of 'dibbling' – dropping the seed potato into a hole made by a stick – the more common practice was to plough them in. As crops flourished, methods of storage were required. Some kept them in a 'tattie-pit', where they were covered by earth to form a mound, and protected from the rain by a layer of turf or other material. Others stored them in a shed or outhouse, where they were stacked against a wall behind wooden slats. Varieties changed regularly as farmers experimented both for taste and size of crop and such grandiose names as Kepplestone Kidneys, Purple Hearts, Duke of Yorks and Arran Chiefs soon became household names on the islands. Home consumption expanded into marketing, adding a new and welcome source of income on the Orkney farm. Few Orcadians, young or old, escaped the back-breaking task of gathering tatties. Using long-pronged forks, men went in front, digging up the crop, while women and children followed behind, diligently picking up each potato and collecting them in a bucket or sack. After several hours a day with bent back, it was a slow and painful business returning to a normal upright posture.

PHOTOGRAPH BY TOM KENT, *c.* 1900

Home-brew was always appreciated during a busy harvest day and Orkney has a long tradition of making good ale. It was the normal thirst-quencher for men and boys and though the degree of alcohol contained in it varied according to the taste of the brewer – usually the woman of the house – it was never looked upon as 'drink'. Its popularity stemmed from the fact that it was cheaper than either milk or tea and it was as much a part of the staple diet as bannocks or brose. Brewing was something of an art and modern techniques have not yet been able to produce a

comparable beverage. The initial preparation of the malt was a complicated process, passed on from generation to generation, and upon its success depended the final product. It was made from bere, barley or corn, which was soaked, spread out on the barn floor, turned over daily until germination began, and then 'stopped', usually by trampling it with the feet. After further germination, it was dried in the kiln, 'winnowed' to clear out the husks and finally ground in the quern. It was considered that a good malt could not be made in under three weeks. A measure of

malt was mixed several times in a vat with quantities of boiled water, each mixture being drawn off as 'wort', and put into a barrel to brew. Hops were added and then the liquid was put to 'barm' by adding yeast. After several days, once fermentation had ceased, it was strained through straw to clear it of sediment and finally bottled and left to settle before it was ready for consumption.

PHOTOGRAPH BY ROBERT H. ROBERTSON, c. 1900

Harvesting, prior to the arrival of machines, was a back-breaking process at the best of times, but when the weather was unfavourable it taxed to the limit the crofter's ingenuity and patience. Small wonder that the Harvest Home Dance and the Harvest Thanksgiving church service were important events in the rural calendar.

Before the advent of the reaper, which began to make its appearance on Orkney farms in the 1890s, the scythe was the main tool for cutting crops. Early scythes had a single long handle with a small grip and a short blade of 15–20 inches, but these gave way to the traditional Scottish type with the much longer blade and the Y-shaped handle. The blade was the vital part and great skill was exercised by the blacksmith in tempering it, usually over a peat-fired forge, and also by the scythesman in honing it to a keen cutting edge. The art of cutting with a scythe was fascinating to watch. The scythesman developed an easy rhythmic swing, which looked deceptively simple, laying the cut grain evenly to one side, making it easy for the women and children following to gather it up and tie it into sheaves. A good scythesman would keep two people lifting and tying.

An indispensable tool long after the arrival of the reaper, the scythe was used to open up 'roads' for the machines and for cutting crop badly flattened or twisted by wind and rain.

PHOTOGRAPH BY TOM KENT, c. 1900

After the scythe came the reaper, and harvesting became a great deal quicker and easier by comparison. It arrived in Orkney at the end of the nineteenth century, and as it developed various types emerged: one-horse, two-horse, side-delivery, back-delivery and self-delivery.

However, the reaper had its limitations and all it replaced was the scythe. Sheaves still had to be handmade. The binder, which followed in the 1920s, was more ambitious, since it tied the sheaves as well, and it became widely used, particularly after the Second World War.

Another major step forward was the use of the tractor, which lead eventually to a large reduction in the farm labour force and the ultimate demise in farm use of that majestic animal, the horse. Here are two stages in the progress of one local farm, overlooking Scapa Flow. The photograph above is a typical harvest scene in the days of the reaper, while the opposite one was taken when the farmer had progressed to a Hornsby binder.

PHOTOGRAPHS BY TOM KENT: ABOVE, *c.* 1900; OPPOSITE, *c.* 1930

56

A field of stooks at harvest time was a satisfying sight. For the passer-by it offered an aesthetically pleasing picture but for the farmer it represented many long hours of back-breaking work. 'Bands' had to be made from a handful of straw and firmly tied round the centre of a bundle of cut grain, with the ends twisted together into a knot, thus forming a sheaf. The sheaves were then set up in pairs, leaning against one another in groups of six or eight to form a stook. When his year's labour had reached this stage, the farmer was, for a time at least, less dependent on the elements.

PHOTOGRAPH BY TOM KENT, *c.* 1900

When the sheaves had dried off, they were carted into the yard and built into weatherproof stacks, ready for threshing when required. Carts and 'sleds' were the normal form of transport, though on smaller crofts sheaves were often carried in on the backs of the crofter and his family. Providing the season had not been a disaster, something that was not uncommon in our uncertain climate, harvest was a happy time, particularly for the children who were allowed special holidays from school to help out.

PHOTOGRAPH BY TOM KENT, *c.* 1910

An improvement on the flail was the small hand-powered threshing mill, which began to appear in Orkney about the 1850s. It was work for at least three people – in this case, two men turning the cranks which rotated the drum inside, with a woman feeding in sheaves and probably clearing the straw from the other end. These small mills were a great boon to the smallholder who could not afford a large power-driven mill. They were often made locally, many being converted to run on wind or water power and later, as mechanisation began to make an impact, some were driven by an old car engine.

PHOTOGRAPH BY DAVID HORNE, *c.* 1900

The grinding of grain is a prehistoric process and has taken many forms over the centuries, from the simple mortar and pestle up to the highly sophisticated grain mills of today. The quernstone, or hand mill, has been used in Orkney for many years, having been introduced to Britain about the time of the Roman occupation. It was still in use here in the twentieth century for grinding small quantities of grain, malt or bere. It consisted of two circular stones, about 21 inches in diameter and from 2 to 2½ inches thick. The upper disc moved while the lower one remained still, often attached to a wooden or stone platform. A wooden handle was fixed to the top stone by which it was rotated as grain was fed through the hole in the centre. The contacting surfaces were picked and roughened to enhance the grinding process. The procedure was heavy going for women and continuous movement was achieved by changing hands. Attempts were made by greedy landowners to ban the practice during the seventeenth century and quernstones were confiscated and broken up, forcing tenants to use the laird's mill and pay the necessary dues.

PHOTOGRAPH BY TOM KENT, *c.* 1900

Powered mills were used in Orkney as early as the fifteenth century. Similar in operation to hand mills, but much larger, they were driven by water, which offered a more constant and controllable source of power or, alternatively, as Orkney is fairly weak in water courses, by wind, something we are not short of. This small windmill is typical of many in Orkney during the nineteenth century. It is not clear whether this one was a threshing mill or a grinding mill but the basic structure of the power source was similar. The number of sails varied from two to eight and the speed was controlled to a certain degree by the number of sails or the amount of canvas offered to the wind source. To stop the mill the sails were turned edge on to the wind and either rolled up or removed. Threshing mills like this were still in operation on the island of Papa Westray in the 1940s.

PHOTOGRAPH BY TOM KENT, *c.* 1900

This mill at Peckhole, on the island of North Ronaldsay, was a turret-post mill, a type unique to Orkney. Reputedly the last wind-powered grain mill to operate in Scotland, it worked up until about 1908, when it was initially replaced by a vertical water mill, and later by one driven by diesel power. The base was almost 12 feet in diameter. The cartwheel arrangement was to assist in turning the mill to face the wind, and the block and tackle to raise the ladder while it was being rotated. The sails were normally rolled up when not in use.

PHOTOGRAPH BY TOM KENT, *c.* 1900

The most important components of any mill were the millstones, between which the grain was ground into meal or flour. Like most stones they were quarried, handcut to the desired size, with a central hole, and then split to the required thickness. They varied in diameter from 30 to 36 inches in smaller mills, up to 6 or 7 feet in larger ones. The truing-up of millstones was a highly skilled process, which had to be undertaken by the miller at regular intervals. This millstone is being quarried at Yesnaby, in the main-island parish of Sandwick, where the gritty texture of the sandstone was considered to be ideal for the purpose. Normal production was about 10 stone per annum, which at the beginning of the twentieth century cost about two shillings per inch thickness at the 'eye'.

PHOTOGRAPH BY ROBERT H. ROBERTSON, *c.* 1900

Water mills were more sophisticated in construction and designed in two basic types – horizontal or vertical, depending on the plane of the power wheel, which in a horizontal mill lies flat in the water course and is attached directly to the millstone above it; in a vertical mill the power wheel is upright and is operated by water directed over the top into 'feathers' or troughs on the surface of the wheel, the weight of water causing it to turn. Examples of the horizontal mill can still be seen in Orkney today. This is the interior of the old 'click-mill' at Birsay on the main island, showing the simple construction of the 'hopper' above to feed the grain through the 'eye' to be ground by the heavy millstone underneath. The ground meal was ejected through the wooden chute in front into the stone box or 'bing' below. This mill was taken over by the Office of Works in 1932. The building is 15 feet in length, 7 feet in width and 5 feet in height.

PHOTOGRAPH BY TOM KENT, c. 1930

Vertical mills were soon to replace the small horizontal type. They gradually developed from small units into the large three-storey buildings, with huge millwheels still widely seen in Orkney today. In both systems the water supply was normally directed from a burn or milldam, along a mill 'lade' on to the wheel, and speed was controlled to a degree by sluicegates which regulated the quantity of water delivered. Dams were constructed to build up the necessary head of water to supply sufficient power and in the case of the vertical mill a gearing system was developed to give greater speeds.

Here at Woodwick Mill in Evie on the main island, the wooden mill 'lade' and the large cast-iron millwheel are clearly seen and the normal course of the burn is in the foreground. The high part on the right of the building is the kiln where grain was dried before grinding. In the background is Woodwick House, for many years the home of the Traill family.

Milling was a seasonal occupation and not even then full time. It depended on the supply of grain and in many cases on the availability of water and was therefore usually confined to the winter months. In 1600 there were over fifty mills operating throughout the islands; now there is only one, at Boardhouse in Birsay on the main island.

PHOTOGRAPH BY TOM KENT, *c. 1900*

66

The largest mill built in Orkney was Ayre Mill in Kirkwall, which stood on the Oyce, the narrow channel between the Peedie Sea and Kirkwall Bay. Constructed originally by Thomas Flett in 1839 as a sawmill, it was operated by a water wheel housed in the building on the right; the wheel turned as the tide ebbed and flowed through the channel below, to and from the Peedie Sea. As well as changing direction the wheel was designed to rise and fall with the tide.

Later the building was converted to a meal mill, evident from the white patches on the walls. It was purchased by James Williamson, who in turn changed its power source to steam. It was last operated as a mill by Robert Garden & Company but it has now been converted into flats and small business units. The water area in the foreground has been filled in as part of the main Kirkwall–Stromness road.

PHOTOGRAPH BY TOM KENT, *c.* 1900

COUNTRY SKILLS

A COUNTRYMAN WAS A MAN OF MANY PARTS. Over the years necessity made him master of many skills, and over the years these skills changed to meet the needs of the time. Apart from his occupational knowledge, which in Orkney has always been mainly concerned with the land or the sea, he had to be able to turn his hand to most aspects of building, in stone, wood or straw, in order to keep his home and outhouses sound. Farmers knew how to fish and fishermen knew how to work the land. Both knew how to obtain additional food for their families by extracting various forms of shellfish from the seashore, by catching auks or other birds, by knowing where to find wild birds' eggs, and by trapping hares or rabbits. Fuel was cut from the land in the form of peat and when an additional source of income presented itself, as during the kelp boom, he learned how to handle seaweed as well. To care for his livestock a certain amount of veterinary knowledge was essential. He was often his own blacksmith and cobbler, and in his spare time he may have been an accomplished musician, poet or homespun philosopher. He was invariably a regular church attender.

The countrywoman was no less accomplished. Her role was different but her skills were just as vital if home and family were to survive. She looked after all that happened inside the house and a good deal of what went on outside, particularly on a croft or farm, where the pigs, poultry, milk and garden were her domain. She had to turn her hand to cooking, baking, sewing, mending, knitting, spinning, even weaving, and brewing. She was usually the family doctor, since on most islands none was available, and many of her home cures or folk remedies have withstood the test of time. She served as wife, mother, daughter, sister, servant and, if necessary, bread-winner as needs dictated.

As a team they had a special relationship, not flamboyant but based on mutual respect, a relationship that was totally interdependent and at one with their environment. They survived on their wits and on the strength of their backs, and when that was not enough, and often it was not, it was no reflection on them but rather on the role in which they were cast. Survival was not always an option.

This well-posed photograph illustrates a number of Orcadian cottage crafts. The woman is knitting a shawl. The wool she is using would have been spun on her own spinning wheel and stored in a basket, probably handmade by her husband, similar in style to a 'caisie' – the traditional all-purpose container. The chair in which she is sitting would also have been homemade in the traditional design of the Orkney chair. On the wall is a cruisie lamp, common in Orkney up until the middle of the nineteenth century. Made locally by a blacksmith, the cruisie had an upper and a lower shell. The upper one contained the oil reservoir, while the lower caught any overflow or drips. The lower shell and back were usually constructed as one, but the upper shell was suspended on a toothed or notched bar to allow the adjustment necessary to keep even the flow of oil to the wick at the front, which was normally made of cotton. The spinning wheel is of the vertical type with a stool base. More compact than the horizontal type, with the flyer and spindle bobbin above the wheel, it was less easily damaged. The wheel was usually small, not more than 16 inches, to prevent the other parts from being uncomfortably high in operation, but this in turn necessitated more treadling. This type of wheel was normally used for flax. The clock on the wall, though common in the isles, was not traditionally Orcadian. It is known as a 'wag-it-awa' or more correctly, a dial clock, mainly German in origin, but widely used throughout Britain. It was driven by weights and controlled by a pendulum, neither of which was enclosed as in a long case clock.

PHOTOGRAPH BY TOM KENT, *c.* 1900

Straw is a material that has been traditionally used in Orkney for all sorts of purposes. It was used in roofing in a form similar to thatch but tied down with 'simmens' or straw ropes. Simmens were used in many ways throughout the house and on the croft or farm as the only form of rope available. Straw was also used in the making of Orkney chairs and stools, for baskets, 'cubbies' and 'caisies'.

The caisie is a general purpose container which was used for carrying peats, groceries, dung, even children – in fact anything which would fit and was capable of being carried. It was invariably the lot of women to carry them, though it was also common to sling caisies in pairs across the back of a pony or ox. The caisie was made by weaving two strands of bent grass simmens alternately between each layer of straw, working upwards in a circular direction. The top edge or 'fesgar' was especially designed to give added strength. In general, the caisie tapers gradually from top to bottom, while a similar and usually smaller container, the cubbie, had parallel sides and a rounded bottom. They were attached to the carrier's back by strong bent bands which were slung over the shoulder or around the chest. The cubbie had an even wider variety of uses – domestic, agricultural and even for fishing – and was usually designed for a particular purpose, such as sowing seed or holding bait, varying in size accordingly.

This photograph shows a caisie under construction, while the one opposite illustrates a caisie in use for carrying peats.

PHOTOGRAPHS BY TOM KENT, c. 1900

70

The making of Orkney chairs or 'stools' is a tradition that is still carried on, though now mainly as a commercial enterprise. The methods have not changed and the materials also remain basically the same, though now the frames are more commonly constructed of hardwoods such as Japanese oak, and the backs from a variety of new breeds of straw as modern crops change. Traditionally they would have been made from the straw of black oats, which was long and supple, while the frames would have been made from any timber that was available, mainly driftwood. Various sizes and styles were produced, some with hoods for additional protection from the draughts that were part of rural cottage life, and some with drawers under the seats. There were chairs designed specially for men, women and children. Working side by side are Robert Foubister and his daughter Lizzie, of Nessie in Tankerness on the main island. Lizzie is cleaning the straw, by removing the oats and husks, a process which, if thoroughly done, took almost as long as constructing the back itself. Her father is building the back from the bottom up, stitching it to the frame as he goes.

PHOTOGRAPH BY TOM KENT, *c.* 1920

72

One of the more fascinating places to visit was the old blacksmith's shop – the sparks, the ringing sound of the hammer and anvil, the strong acrid smells of peat, coke or burning hooves, the imposing physical presence of large work horses in a confined space and the lively drama when one played up while being shod. It never seemed to be tidy, though everything would have been in its appointed place; metal, dust and cobwebs were everywhere, from flagstone floor to roof. This smithy had two forges, a fairly sophisticated arrangement of lifting tackle for heavy items, and for some unknown reason, an open roof. A wide range of tools is in evidence, the sheet-metal store can be seen in the background, and the paraffin flask for getting the fire going.

PHOTOGRAPH BY TOM KENT, *c.* 1900

Spinning came to a peak in Orkney as a commercial enterprise during the latter half of the eighteenth and the early part of the nineteenth centuries, though it was practised before and after this period. This was as the result of a boom in the linen trade and it became for a time a major industry here. It was highly profitable for the few who ran it and also a welcomed additional income for women. Flax was grown here, but when it did not suffice it was imported. It was spun into yarn, a job requiring great skill, woven into cloth or knitted into stockings, and then exported to Newcastle upon Tyne, Edinburgh, Glasgow and other southern markets. The linen trade employed spinners, weavers, flax dressers and dyers.

About 1800, one enterprising merchant employed a woman to teach the art of spinning and some 200 girls were trained. At the Lammas Market during this period, trade in linen was extensive. To give some idea of the production: on the main island, Deerness alone provided 20,000 yards of the material in 1805 and in Kirkwall around 1790 there were fifty-three weavers, eight journeymen weavers, and fourteen apprentices. One other benefit to the community was that linen was commonly accepted in lieu of land rent and often was the difference for many crofters between survival and going under.

This treadle wheel is of the earlier horizontal type commonly used in the eighteenth century.

PHOTOGRAPH BY TOM KENT, *c.* 1900

Though not a traditional cottage industry in Orkney, weaving has been practised here for many years. In earlier days each parish had its own weaver producing blankets and broadcloth for suits. It became commercially viable during the late eighteenth and early nineteenth centuries with the boom years of the linen trade, and again between the two world wars when Robert Garden, who had business interests in the Western Isles, brought over a number of skilled weavers from there and set up several looms in his premises in Laing Street for the production of tweed. As the demand grew, larger accommodation was required, firstly, in part of their Bridge Street/Garden Street store, and later in the old Volunteer Hall in Junction Road, where twelve looms were in operation up to twelve hours per day. John Sclater also began weaving on a large scale after the Second World War but by the 1960s a combination of the introduction of power looms and a drop in the market for tweed eventually closed both businesses. Now it is carried out by individuals on a small scale. This photograph is unusual because David M. Kirkness, better known as an Orkney chair maker, is at the loom. It could be that he experimented for a time with an alternative craft, or simply that he built this loom for a customer. It must have been only a transitory interest since he never appeared in the local trade directories as a weaver. Evidence of his normal stock in trade can be seen all around, with a stack of timber on the right, straw hanging down from the loft and carpenters' tools in the background.

PHOTOGRAPH BY TOM KENT, *c.* 1910

There is an abundance of seaweed around Orkney's shores. Though for many centuries harvested for use as fertiliser, its commercial value as kelp or burnt seaweed was first realised here during the eighteenth century and this aspect of it is believed to have been explored initially on the island of Stronsay in 1722. It provided a valuable source of iodine and potassium salts for the country, a profitable new source of income for landlords and more importantly, for crofting tenants, an additional means of employment and income. There was for a time some opposition to the process from the fishing industry, which claimed that it drove fish away and also, since about 3,000 people were employed in it during the summer months, deprived the fishing industry of much of its work force. Farms and crofts also tended to be neglected. In 1740 the income was declared at around £2,000 but by 1793 this had risen to £17,000. The biggest recorded yield was in 1825 at 3,500 tons. Most of the kelp was shipped to Newcastle upon Tyne. The industry dwindled gradually over the nineteenth and the early part of the twentieth centuries and eventually fell into total decline. There was an attempt to revive it after the Second World War and residents in Kirkwall can well remember the unpleasant smell when the wind was blowing from the north-west.

The process was fairly tedious and not very pleasant. From mid-November onwards, tangles were cut with sickles and spread out on the grass or laid on stone 'steethes' to dry. It was then

turned occasionally to prevent fermentation and
finally it was burned on a kelp kiln. The ash was
left to cool into a solid mass and then broken up
for transport.

The two photographs illustrate kelp-making in
the parish of Birsay on the main island: the one
opposite, showing a handbarrow, which consists
simply of two long poles with cross spars to
support the seaweed, and the one above is of a
woman tending a kelp kiln.

PHOTOGRAPHS BY TOM KENT, *c.* 1900

Peat-cutting has been carried out in Orkney since prehistoric times. Though the Earl of Orkney Turf-Einar was given credit for its introduction in the ninth century – hence his name – archaeological evidence indicates that it was in use here long before that. It was the common domestic fuel of Orkney, in both town and country, but on the island of Eday, where the peat was of particularly good quality, it developed as an industry in the 1840s, reaching a peak between 1860 and 1870.

The top turf was cut into squares with a 'ritting knife' – a long curved blade – and removed with a turf spade, seen on the left of the photograph above. The peat was then cut with one of two types of tools, the 'tusker' or the 'luggie'. Men usually did the cutting and women lifted the peats out. Great care and skill were exercised in cutting the bank properly, often to a depth of several peats. After a few days the peats were spread out on the grass, to be 'raised' later into small groups, and if necessary, 'rooed' into larger mounds until thoroughly dried out. Finally, they were brought to the roadside and transported home, either

manually in wheelbarrows or 'caisies' or carted by horse or ox, and built into peat stacks, carefully constructed to run off water when it rained.

These methods remain largely unchanged though now, of course, motorised vehicles are used for bringing the peats home. The amount of work involved was dictated largely by the weather. In a good year comparatively little effort was required but in a wet summer it was always a struggle to get the peats dried and out of the hill before the weather broke. The quality varied immensely from place to place. The soft brown

'foggy' or 'yarpha' peat lasted no time on the fire and to have rights to a bank with hard black peat was a great asset. Certain hill areas around Kirkwall were set aside for residents to cut their winter fuel. Large commercial consumers of peat are the two local distilleries, who use it to dry the barley for making whisky in order to give it its particular flavour.

PHOTOGRAPHS BY TOM KENT: OPPOSITE, *c.* 1900; ABOVE, *c.* 1920

The day the peats were carted home from the hill was an important one in the crofter's calendar. It meant that one of the season's many essential chores was completed and the winter fuel safely at hand. It was an event that had to be fitted into a fairly tight yearly schedule, in suitable weather, and it was therefore not uncommon to find almost the entire parish carting peats on the same day. This photograph was taken on such a day in Birsay on the main island.

PHOTOGRAPH BY TOM KENT, *c. 1900*

Catching 'spoots' or razor fish has been practised in Orkney for centuries, mainly through necessity, as all forms of 'ebb-meat' played an important part in the staple diet of Orcadians. Even now, when most people can afford their daily bread, many eat spoots regularly, simply because they like them. To reach them, very low tides are required, and they are only suitable for eating at certain times of the year – a simple guide being the months which contain the letter *r*.

Beginners rarely catch many, as the slightest movement on the sand's surface sends the razor fish scuttling downwards. Early successes usually come from walking backwards with back bent and eyes down, so that when the weight disturbs the spoot, its initial movement leaves a small hole and a quick reaction will get it before it burrows too deep. A long-bladed knife slid sideways into the sand to touch the shell is enough to stop it and it can then be dug out. Many cut fingers come from this practice, for they are not named razor fish without reason. The experts walk normally, forward and upright, in the sure knowledge that they can recognise the small indentation formed on the sand's surface by the presence of a spoot, and they can pluck it out efficiently with the fingers before it gets a chance to move.

Cooking is simple. They are run under the tap to remove sand and then dipped in boiling water to open the shells. The 'fruit' are then extracted, seasoned and little more than warmed in a frying pan. They are then ready for the table. This local delicacy is normally eaten by the dozen or even by the score.

PHOTOGRAPH BY DAVID HORNE, *c.* 1905

The precarious art of 'auk-swapping' was a traditional and necessary activity, particularly on the island of Westray, where auks are to be found in abundance at certain times of the year. The catcher had to climb down the cliffs to a suitable position, using no equipment other than home-made straw ropes or 'simmens'. He took with him a large net on the end of a long pole, which he used to 'swap' or catch auks, mostly in flight. The birds were taken home and eaten, the feathers used for pillows and the bones used as fertiliser. Nothing was wasted. Auks' eggs were also taken for food. Here is Thomas Rendall of Longhouse in Westray 'swapping' auks at Noup Head, a cliff standing almost 240 feet above sea level.

PHOTOGRAPH BY ROBERT H. ROBERTSON, *c.* 1912

HAMNAVOE

THE TOWN OF STROMNESS, meaning 'the Ness projecting into the rapid stream' (Hoy Sound), lies in the parish of the same name on the south-west corner of the main island of Orkney. About one-third the size of Kirkwall, it is the only other town in Orkney and has a population of around 2,000 to Kirkwall's 6,700. With the hills of the island of Hoy forming a spectacular backdrop, this picturesque little hamlet straggles along the coast for about a mile, many of its houses standing end on to the waterfront, with gables dropping directly into the sea. It is a warren of narrow closes, alleys and side streets, many leading down to the jetties and slip-ways that abound along its foreshore. Traditionally known by its old Norse name, Hamnavoe, meaning 'haven bay', the harbour has been a safe anchorage for many centuries. Used by the Vikings during their period in Orkney, over the years it has also sheltered ocean liners, fishing fleets, cargo ships, whalers, the transport ships of the Hudson's Bay Company, lighthouse tenders, warships and even seaplanes. Changing little as time passed, with its narrow winding main street, lined by stone houses with their crow-stepped gables, happily its character is now being rigidly maintained through strict building controls.

A popular and picturesque view of Stromness,
taken from the South End, shows the many piers
and houses along the waterfront. The Lighthouse
Pier was built in the 1890s. The shore has been a
playground for children since the town began and
an ability with boats, learned from an early age,
has led many to a seafaring life.

PHOTOGRAPH BY TOM KENT, *c.* 1910

This beautiful view of snow-capped Stromness is
taken from Brinkie's Brae, the hill which
dominates the town. The old ship's hulk, furthest
out from the shore, was used by William
Sutherland as a coal store.

PHOTOGRAPH BY TOM KENT, c. 1900

An early view of Victoria Street. The first shop on the left was a draper's shop owned by William Duff and is now solicitor J.E.P. Robertson's office. Beyond it was the Commercial Hotel, now partly occupied by a chip shop, and one shop further on was another draper's shop belonging to John G. Johnston. The building on the right with the group outside it was to become the photographer Robert H. Robertson's grocery shop and is now R.S. Merriman's electrical shop. The Mason's Arms Hotel ran for many years under various owners, before becoming the Oakleigh Hotel. The owner at the time of the photograph was John Mackay, who also later built the Kirkwall Hotel, the Stromness Hotel and the Standing Stones Hotel. The coach in the picture was clearly designed for public use rather than private, and may have been one of John Mackay's coaches, which operated along the 14-mile stretch between Stromness and Kirkwall.

PHOTOGRAPH BY GEORGE W. WILSON, c. 1890

This quaint part of Stromness, which lies behind numbers sixteen and eighteen Dundas Street, has remained almost untouched over the years. Like many other houses in the town, it is still possible to fish for 'sillocks' or young saithe from a window at high tide.

PHOTOGRAPH BY GEORGE W. WILSON, *c.* 1890

This attractive part of Stromness foreshore lies behind David C. Tower's house and shop, as viewed from Sutherland's Pier. Some of the many private slipways can be seen. Also in evidence are various private sewage exits, which appeared between 1911 and 1914 when individual proprietors were 'encouraged' to adhere to the sanitary inspector's recommendations to install proper water and sewage facilities in their houses. The opening in the garden wall to the left of centre leading apparently to the sea was originally the access to a corrugated iron toilet which was suspended out over the water. This was not an unusual practice in dwellings next to the waterfront. The 'Power Petrol' sign was undoubtedly placed to attract shipping as it approached Stromness Harbour.

PHOTOGRAPH BY TOM KENT, *c.* 1920

88

A busy moment in Dundas Street, before Samuel Leask's shop in Graham Place was removed. The men waiting expectantly on the left were standing outside the public house then owned by the Watt family, who also had a brewery up 'Pigeon's Creek', off Graham Place. This small corner of the town has changed little in essence since this photograph was taken.

PHOTOGRAPH BY GEORGE W. WILSON, *c.* 1890

89

John Rae's shop in Stromness is over 100 years old and is now under the ownership of The Leonards, Kirkwall. It remains as a newsagent and stationers, with fancy goods and toys. The window displays give an indication of the range of goods sold – toys, dolls, games, musical instruments, leather goods, schoolbags, picture frames, jewellery, walking sticks, greetings cards, books and, surprisingly, expensive Goss china.

The postcards outside were produced by the photographer Tom Kent. At the time this photograph was taken, the shop also acted as a booking agent for various shipping lines concerned with emigration.

PHOTOGRAPH BY ROBERT H. ROBERTSON, *c*. 1900

Queen Street is now incorporated into the Back Road. The notion that it may have been built by, and for, French prisoners after the Napoleonic Wars, along with many of the dykes around Stromness, is now considered by many to be doubtful. All the houses, apart from one, were demolished about 1911. Note the unusual stonework and the varied use of flagstones, turf and 'simmens' or straw ropes in the construction of the roofs.

PHOTOGRAPH BY GEORGE W. WILSON, *c.* 1890

DISTILLERY AND OLD TOWN HALL, STROMNESS.

Stromness Distillery, the building on the left, was first in operation in 1817 under John Crookshanks, producing spirits under the name of Man o' Hoy. It passed through various hands until its final owner J. & J. McConnell Limited made it famous with a very fine malt whisky called Old Orkney. In 1890 the distillery recorded an output of 7,000 gallons and had two bonded warehouses containing 300 casks. It ceased production in 1928 and was demolished in 1940. Mayburn Court, an attractive new housing scheme built to follow the outline of the old distillery, now stands on the site. The distinguished author George Mackay Brown resides here.

Stromness Town Hall, in the centre, was built in 1858 and upstairs housed the museum of the Orkney Natural History Society. When the hall was moved to new premises in Hellihole, the museum expanded into the ground floor and is currently about to add the house on the extreme right for additional display space. The large B sign protruded from the premises of Edward Baikie, boat builder. This good example of an Orkney yole (on the right) was presumably 'dry-docked' for winter.

The photograph opposite shows the distillery in 1940 with demolition work in progress.

PHOTOGRAPHS: ABOVE ATTRIBUTED TO GEORGE W. WILSON, c. 1890; OPPOSITE BY WILLIAM HOURSTON, c. 1940

The Lighthouse Pier was built in the 1890s by the Northern Lighthouse Board to berth the series of ships *Pharos* and *Pole Star*, which have been used over the years to service the many lighthouses, beacons and buoys that protect shipping in Orkney and Shetland waters. The Stromness depot, and the houses for the board's staff, still exist, playing an important part in the employment of the town. The Lighthouse Board was established in 1786 as a result of an Act of Parliament and the first lighthouse to be built in Orkney was the old North Ronaldsay light in 1789, designed and constructed by Robert Stevenson and Thomas Smith, pioneers in this field. In all, twelve major lights and eleven minor were erected, almost all of them automatically operated now. The flagstones being dressed for surfacing the pier were probably taken from Liddle's Quarry in Orphir on the main island.

PHOTOGRAPH BY ROBERT H. ROBERTSON, *c.* 1895

Until this extension, constructed during 1893 and 1894, the South Pier was an open structure; to give it additional stability, the decision was taken to clad it in stone at the same time. The photograph shows, as well as the workmen and their materials, the diving boat used for underwater work and the cranes used for moving the heavy blocks. The stores on the pier were also extended to cope with increasing traffic. In the background stands Garson Farm.

PHOTOGRAPH ATTRIBUTED TO TOM KENT, *c.* 1894

THE ROYAL BURGH

KIRKWALL, FROM THE OLD NORSE NAME, KIRKJUVÁGR, meaning 'church bay', is believed to be named after the small church dedicated to St Olaf, which was in existence before St Magnus Cathedral, its doorway still to be seen in St Olaf's Wynd. It is the capital town of the islands and a royal burgh since 1486. A market town, with a current population of about 6,700, it sprawls around its focal point, St Magnus Cathedral. Kirkwall's history is steeped in the fluctuating fortunes and powers of the Orkney earls and bishops, whose palaces lie within the cathedral precincts, where in those sacred shadows many unholy and violent deeds have been enacted. Cosmetic alterations have changed, to a degree, the façade of Kirkwall's main street but the character of the older parts of the town remains essentially intact. Before preference was given to Scapa Flow, Kirkwall Bay offered safe anchorage to warships of many nations, including those of the Norwegian King Hakon Hakonson on his ill-fated expedition in 1263; German ships prior to the First World War; United States navy minesweepers during the period immediately after that war; and, on many occasions, the various units of our own navy. Not as picturesque as Stromness, Kirkwall has, all the same, a charm of its own.

This excellent view of Kirkwall, taken from Ayre Road, shows the Peedie Sea when it stretched up to the old gasworks site on Junction Road (on the right). Today there is no water to be seen from this angle, the whole area having been reclaimed and buildings erected. The in-filling for Samuel Baikie's woodyard has not yet begun, and St Magnus Cathedral is in its pre-restoration state, with short spire and old turret and clock. The gasworks have now gone, replaced by a sheltered-housing scheme. Access to the Peedie Sea in earlier times was through the Oyce channel and it was used regularly for the shelter, repair and building of boats. It was also used for transporting goods like peats to private houses, or for floating in timber for William B. Peace's sawmills (on the left).

PHOTOGRAPH BY GEORGE W. WILSON, *c.* 1890

A view of Kirkwall, looking north-west from the tower of St Magnus Cathedral. On the left is the Peedie Sea, bounded by the sea walls, a substantial area of which was reclaimed to accommodate many of the buildings along Junction Road today. On the point of land at the top left-hand corner the old Kirkwall–Stromness road is clearly visible, bending through Hatston Farm before it was diverted to make room for an aerodrome during the First World War. Stacks of timber in W.B. Peace's woodyard are to be seen just above centre on the site where Kirkwall Post Office now stands, and the tall masts of several sailing ships rise up from the harbour. The twin gables just left of centre belonged to the Castle Hotel, now the Social Club of the Occidental Oil Consortium, and directly across from it lies the site on which the Masonic Hall was to be opened in 1887. The street between is Castle Street, constructed in 1865 to give improved access to Kirkwall Harbour. This caused the removal of the last remaining vestiges of the old Kirkwall Castle from the area immediately in front of the Castle Hotel, a castle which had been the stronghold of Henry St Clair, Earl of Orkney in the fourteenth century, and from which the much detested Robert Stewart, Earl of Orkney, was taken prisoner in 1614 after a siege conducted on behalf of the Scottish Government by George Sinclair, Earl of Caithness. Stewart was subsequently tried and executed in Edinburgh for his many tyrannous deeds. The shop on the extreme bottom left of the picture was to become the premises of Tom Kent, producer of many of the fine photographs in this book.

PHOTOGRAPH BY GEORGE W. WILSON, *c.* 1880

98

Under the Kirkwall Harbour Act of 1828, the Kirkwall Harbour Trustees held their first meeting on 17 June of that year, under the chairmanship of Provost Samuel Laing. The main item on the agenda was the extension of the East Pier, which was put into effect over the next three years. In 1838 the brick-built navigation light was erected at a cost of £22.14s.11d. By 1855 traffic had increased immensely and the lengthening of the pier was discussed but nothing was done. The subject came up regularly and eventually led to the Kirkwall Harbour Act of 1859, at which time the East Pier measured 560 feet and the West Pier 360 feet, but still no action was taken until 1862. Between 1865 and 1867 the new iron pier was designed by R. Denison of London and constructed by R. Laidlaw & Son, Glasgow, at a cost of £12,000. In 1865 another major alteration affecting the pier was the removal of old buildings from Harbour Street to widen the street, and the construction of the access roads, Junction Road and Castle Street. By 1871 the new Harbour Office was built. In 1874 additional berthing accommodation was required and the iron pier was giving some cause for concern as to its stability. Plans were prepared by John D. Miller, Kirkwall, and the work was completed in 1886 at a total cost of £17,500. At the time the harbour was considered to be 'one of the most commodious and complete' in Scotland. This photograph shows the open iron pier just prior to the 1886 alterations. The brick lighthouse has gone now and the whole structure has been filled in and widened, and new stores built. Current plans will involve a major development to cater for roll-on-roll-off facilities and an area for loading and off-loading lorries.

PHOTOGRAPH BY GEORGE W. WILSON, c. 1885

In Albert Street William Bews's shop is still a
grocery shop, now under the name of Cumming
and Spence; James Flett's premises next door
were for many years the ironmonger's shop of
Peter C. Flett before recently becoming a cookery
shop; Shearer & Sclater's business continued
under the proprietorship of John Sclater up until
1982, when it was bought over by Mackay's; the
victualling house next door, probably run by
Janet Sclater, became part of Sclater's drapery
shop. On the left-hand side of the street the
building with the bay window, currently

Trenabie's Cafe, was a lodging house or
refreshment room owned by Mrs T. Marwick.
The clearly signposted Albert Lane is now known
as Mounthoolie Lane. The street-sweeper,
complete with barrow and heather brush, has just
passed by a bare-footed boy in straw boater
carrying a milk pail and equally intent on the
business of the day.

PHOTOGRAPHER UNKNOWN, c. 1880, COPIED BY
TOM KENT

A view of Bridge Street, looking towards the harbour. There was plenty of accommodation on offer in this area, strategically placed next to the pier, and a great deal of it appears to have belonged to Mrs Harcus. Her property was taken over by James Flett as a general store and his new Anchor Buildings were established on this site in 1904. Corsie's Temperance Hotel has long since disappeared but Elizabeth Corsie continued to keep lodgers up until after the Second World War. The traditional features of stone walls, grey slates and crow-stepped gables are evident. The cobbled surface has, of course, been removed.

PHOTOGRAPH BY TOM KENT, *c.* 1897

GARDEN, DRAPER, KIRKWALL

Robert Garden, an Aberdonian, came to Orkney intent on starting a business. Initially, he opened a simple grocery shop in Victoria Street, which progressed to a general store in Harbour Street, before finally, in 1892, moving to Bridge Street, occupying a property which had been the town house of the Traill family of Woodwick and later James Conner's Hotel. By the beginning of the twentieth century his was the largest shop-and-warehouse complex in Orkney. It had separate departments for drapery, china, shoes, groceries, a large seeds and manure store, a

lemonade factory, a meal mill and later, a weaving business. It had a branch in Orphir, also on the main island, several horse-drawn and motorised vans and lorries, and a shop boat which called round the outer islands. After 1916, when Robert Garden's widow retired from the business, it came under the control of J. & J. Tod & Son. In 1938 a serious fire, the worst ever in Orkney, destroyed all the main shops, leaving only the seeds store at the rear. Lack of water pressure contributed greatly to the disaster and firefighters had to work extremely hard to

prevent the fire from spreading to adjacent properties, in particular the newly opened Shell Mex oil depot nearby. An estimated £12,000-worth of damage was done and though the original intention was to rebuild as soon as possible, this, in fact, was never done. The business still operates as a wholesale warehouse and bakery, occupying part of the old store, while the remaining area is now a hardware store run independently, and where the shops once stood there is parking space for these two businesses. This photograph shows some of the staff

outside the original drapery, and the one above
shows Robert Garden's car at the petrol pumps
behind the main shops at the entrance to the
seeds store.

PHOTOGRAPHS: OPPOSITE BY UNKNOWN
PHOTOGRAPHER, *c.* 1900; ABOVE BY
TOM KENT, *c.* 1920

The old market or 'mercat' cross, now replaced by a replica, in front of St Magnus Cathedral. Though dated 1621 – the time of its restoration by Bishop George Grahame – it is believed to be much older. It was transferred from its original site in 1762. The original, made of red freestone, is now housed in the gallery of the cathedral. It served many purposes throughout its history. It was often used as a place of punishment – to testify that it was a necessary sacred duty that had to be administered by the magistrates and that no cruelty was intended, criminals were branded there, and it was also used as a pillory, prisoners being chained to it by iron collars or 'jougs'. Before written contracts became commonplace, an agreement was considered binding if made while touching the cross. It has always been, and still is, the place in Kirkwall where proclamations are made.

The two-storey building in the background to the left of the Covenanters' Memorial, situated behind the cross, housed the old Kirkwall Burgh School, before it was declared unsuitable in 1764. The large house, behind and immediately on the right of the cross, was known as the Chaplain's Chamber or the Episcopal Meeting House. Prior to the seventeenth century it served as a manse for the Subdean of the cathedral, before passing through the hands of several prominent Orcadian gentlemen, as a private dwelling house, until it was eventually bought by Lieutenant John Baikie RN in 1821. In 1825 he opened Kirkwall's first banking agency there, the National Bank of Scotland. The bank was later transferred across the street to the building with steps leading to the door, now owned by the Royal Bank of Scotland, and the original house was demolished in 1930 to create wider access to Victoria Street.

PHOTOGRAPH BY TOM KENT, c. 1900

Thanks to the skills of Tom Kent we still have this rare early photograph of Broad Street. It illustrates the method of transporting water for domestic use from the public pump, in a 'say' or a large wooden tub carried by a pole or 'say tree' which passed through holes in the end staves. In 1863 this pump was considered to be unhygienic and by 1871 it was declared by Dr Stevenson Macadam to be unfit for ordinary purposes, requiring closure.

James Kirkness opened his wine shop (next door to J. Matches) in 1859 and this business continued as a licensed grocer in partnership with the Gorie family until 1980. P. McGuire (two doors to the right of the wine shop) still had a watchmaker's shop in Union Street up until 1882 and his shop in Broad Street continued in this line under various proprietors until the last owner William Brough retired in 1969. It is now part of the Longship jewellery and gift shop. The other shops, J. Matches, C. Smith and Thomas Bews (next door to the wine shop) have long since gone, leaving no record of their businesses. The prevailing head gear at this time seems to have been tall hats for men and tam-o'-shanters for boys.

PHOTOGRAPHER UNKNOWN, *c.* 1860, COPIED BY TOM KENT

A view of St Catherine's Place. These working-class houses were built about 1804 by David Drever on an area of land called St Catherine's Quoys, which he had purchased at the time for that purpose. The rental income generated by St Catherine's Quoys was originally dedicated to the support of St Catherine's altar in St Magnus Cathedral, and later to help uphold the cathedral and the parish school.

Wooden gutters were strategically placed to collect rain water in barrels for washing purposes, and the old gas lamp provided what meagre light there was in winter. During summer, smocks and straw-boaters seemed to be the dress for young girls and on a warm day the sun-baked flagstones would have been greatly appreciated.

PHOTOGRAPH BY TOM KENT, *c.* 1900

The entrance to Victoria Street. The building on the left was originally the Chaplain's Chamber, attached to St Magnus Cathedral, and was removed in 1930 to give improved access to the street. The building on the right, behind the railings, was the National (now Royal) Bank of Scotland. Immediately beyond it is a very old property, first recorded in 1692 when it was sold by Patrick Prince to Thomas Louttit of Lyking, Sandwick, Provost of Kirkwall. By 1796 it belonged to Thomas Balfour of Elwick on the island of Shapinsay, who sold it to James Scarth, who turned it into a shop and opened up the door on the east gable giving direct access from the street. He also operated as agent for the first Union Bank in Kirkwall. Later it became the home and surgery of Dr Stewart and continued in this capacity under several doctors until the new Health Centre opened in 1973. The next building was a private dwelling in 1798, when Magnus Anderson set up a bookbinding business, concentrating on Bibles and Psalm books, which he sold at the Lammas Market. His son James trained as a printer at Heriot's Printing Office in Leith, Edinburgh, and on his return he set up a hand press and began the first printing establishment in Kirkwall, where, among other things, he produced the first catalogue of the Orkney Library. His son James began the *Orcadian*, our first local newspaper, in 1854; it still appears regularly each week. The man in the bowler hat is believed to be James Anderson, jun.; one of his printers, dressed in the white apron, is across the street.

PHOTOGRAPH BY GEORGE W. WILSON, *c.* 1890

'The Burn' is still in existence but most of its character has now gone. The buildings on the left were replaced by George Rendall's large drapery store in 1905, still operating under new ownership. The buildings on the right have been extensively renovated and have served variously as an electrical shop, a gents' hairdresser, and currently, as a sports shop. The winding effect of this lane was lost when the wall and buildings behind it on the right-hand side were demolished to make room for a modern concrete car park. The two public water pumps would indicate that the one on the right was replaced by the 'modern' one on the left. The cobbles in the foreground were replaced as the motorcar took over from the horse. One interesting feature of this lane was that almost half of it was roofed over as an air-raid shelter during the Second World War.

PHOTOGRAPH BY TOM KENT, *c.* 1900

On the left of Victoria Street, with street-lamp attached, is the Royal Hotel, and the shop next to it was the tinsmith's shop of John Rendall & Son. The space on the right foreground is now occupied by William H.B. Sutherland's pharmacy. The cobbles, designed to stop horses slipping, have been replaced and many of the shops upgraded but the general appearance of the street remains unchanged. The various lanes branching off to the right – Gunn's Close, Fraser's Close, Warren's Walk and so on – have provided housing for many Kirkwallians over the years.

PHOTOGRAPH BY TOM KENT, *c.* 1910

Before the construction of the new reservoir in 1907 at Wideford Hill, there was a constant demand in Kirkwall for additional water and in particular clean water. There was a supply of sorts, laid between 1876 and 1879 by the Edinburgh firm Leslie & Reid, tapped mainly from springs in the Papdale valley, which was gravity fed to pumps for public use. This was augmented later by springs in other areas and, finally, by a 300-foot bore-hole on the south side of town. Examinations showed that the supply had become contaminated, mainly from the ground through which it flowed, and was therefore unfit for human consumption. Those who did not have private wells had to draw water for washing from the various pumps, and for drinking from springs or from the water cart.

The cart is taking the short cut back to town across the Peedie Sea at low tide. The spring from which it has come was still in use, mainly for hospital patients or invalids at home, until the new landscaping scheme for the Peedie Sea was started in the 1960s.

PHOTOGRAPH BY TOM KENT, *c.* 1900

Grain Farm was situated mainly within the town of Kirkwall. The farm buildings stood at the bottom of Wellington Street, behind the area now occupied by James Dowell's monumental sculptor's yard and the warehouse belonging to Scapa Knitwear Limited. The road in the foreground is still in use, leading to private housing on the right, and most of the buildings and wall on the left remain in whole or in part. The sheep have been brought in for shearing, which can be seen in progress in the background.

PHOTOGRAPH BY TOM KENT, *c.* 1900

Operations at the 300-foot bore-hole
on the south side of Kirkwall raised
hopes that the water question would
at last be settled. However, contam-
ination meant that water once again
had to be drawn from private wells,
pumps and springs, until the new
reservoir was constructed in 1907.

PHOTOGRAPH BY DAVID HORNE,
c. 1900

GETTING ABOUT

TRANSPORT IN ORKNEY HAS EVOLVED ALONG THE SAME LINES as other island communities throughout Britain. Since the invention of the wheel, mobile land transport, pulled by horse or ox, improved to a very high degree of sophistication, before having to give way to engine-driven vehicles designed to suit all purposes. As an island community, the sea was our only link with the outside world until the first air services began here in 1933. The tales of great ships, of shipwrecks, of the amazing feats of rescue, and of the tragedies that befell households and parishes in Orkney would fill many books. The development and expansion of our piers and harbours, our roads and airfields, make fascinating reading. We are lucky that some of our best photographers, particularly Tom Kent, were around at a time of great change to record for us the arrival of the first motorcar and the first aeroplane, to remind us of that exciting, yet sad, transition period when the majestic sailing ships slowly bowed out in favour of the faster and more reliable steamers.

A shopping expedition that should have been enjoyed by this young family but, for one at least, appears not to have been a total success. Most children would have had to walk all the way there and back with no concession for the length of legs, unless they were lucky enough to be despatched on their own, with message bag, purse and shopping list – then time meant nothing and a single errand could take a whole morning. This simple barrow would have doubled as a pram when required, still leaving ample room for messages, milk pail and a couple of small passengers.

PHOTOGRAPH BY DAVID HORNE, *c.* 1900

The primitive ox-drawn cart or 'sled' was used
only in some of Orkney's southern islands. This
one was owned by James Wilson of Flaghill on
the island of Graemsay. The solid wheels were
made of wood with iron bands and braking was
effected by chains which locked the wheels and
prevented them from turning.

PHOTOGRAPH BY TOM KENT, *c.* 1900

A woman, complete with shopping basket, making a purchase from one of the many horse-drawn shop vans which operated throughout the Orkney Islands for many years. As an extension of the country general merchant and supplying everything that was likely to be asked for, they made their daily rounds, providing a great service to a busy rural community. These men were experts in stowing the maximum amount of goods in the minimum of space and offered a local daily news service that was as effective as a CB radio. On this van are pails, rope, forks, hoe handles, and bottles of paraffin and methylated spirits filled from the cans below. On the roof, reached by a ladder at the front, there are sacks, probably containing bran, maize or oil cake and other larger items, including a wheelbarrow, which would have been for use rather than for sale. Inside were groceries and other perishables. These vans gave way to motorised vehicles, which have also all but disappeared from the Orkney scene, replaced by the attractions of the supermarket and the convenience of the motor-car. One additional service that these vans provided in Orkney for a time was the delivery of the library's 'family boxes', particularly in the outer isles where mobile libraries were not practicable.

PHOTOGRAPH BY TOM KENT, *c.* 1900

Boat launches in Kirkwall were a common enough event in past years but they never failed to attract a large audience. Though the fishing industry has fluctuated dramatically in Orkney over the years, the ownership of a boat has always held a high priority in the community and many boat-building businesses have prospered here. This fishing smack, *Hemarin*, is being pulled from the yard of George Hercus on 12 March 1885. This operation involved the use of rollers, a traction engine and many willing hands as it was manoeuvred from the yard along Harbour Street and Shore Street and down the ramp on to the shore below Cromwell Road, where it was manhandled into the sea. Built for five Faroese fishermen for use in Faroese and Icelandic waters, she was 56 feet long, with a beam of 15 feet 8 inches, a 7-foot-deep hold, and registered at 22 tons. The sails were also made in Kirkwall by D. Hercus, probably a relative, and the naming ceremony was performed by George Hercus's wife. Fitting-out was expected to have been completed in a few days and her crew were in Orkney ready to sail her north.

This area of Kirkwall has changed. The buildings in the centre remain, though much improved, as Pat Sutherland's electrical shop, but the yard is now a car park behind the Albert Hotel, not yet built when this photograph was taken.

PHOTOGRAPHER UNKNOWN, 1885, COPIED BY TOM KENT

On 9 August 1907 the three-masted schooner *Celtic* of Chester, bound from London to Oban on the Scottish west coast, with a load of cement, was wrecked on the Point of Verran, Bay of Skaill, Sandwick, on the main island. Several gales and heavy seas had rendered her helpless, when she lost her fore topmast, with topsail, topgallant, yards and some headsails. Including Captain Hall, the crew of six, wearing cork jackets, managed with help to struggle safely ashore, and found shelter in the houses of residents, where medical attention was administered to the injured. The *Celtic* was an iron ship, registered at 175 tons, and owned by Captain Hall in partnership with his father and uncle in Arklow, Ireland.

PHOTOGRAPH BY ROBERT H. ROBERTSON, *c.* 1907

One of the many fine ship studies
taken by Tom Kent. Unfortunately,
the name of this beautiful three-
master, moored in Kirkwall Harbour,
is not recorded but she seems to hail
from Denmark.

PHOTOGRAPH BY TOM KENT, *c.* 1900

The west side of the West Pier in Kirkwall was a favourite spot for dry-docking ships for maintenance or repair work. Cleaning, painting, tarring, caulking and the repair of minor damage were carried out regularly, particularly during periods of extreme tides. The *Enchantress*, on the right, was originally built as a fishing smack at Hull in 1878, registered at 67 tons. She was bought in 1889 by Peter Craigie of Kirkwall, who converted her to a coaster. On 3 November 1919 she was wrecked near Peterhead and though she became a total loss, fortunately her crew were all rescued.

PHOTOGRAPH BY DAVID HORNE, *c.* 1900

The old iron paddle steamer *Pharos V* served the Northern Lighthouse Board for thirty-six years. Based at Granton on mainland Scotland she was used mainly for carrying supplies and making the required annual inspection of lights and beacons under the Board's control. She was built in 1874 to replace *Pharos IV* by R. Napier & Company Limited, Glasgow, and measured 205 feet with a 27-foot beam, weighing 574 tons and with engines that generated 353 horsepower. She was apparently a very comfortable ship, praised by the several commissioners and 'guests', who took their free annual trip to Orkney and Shetland, as offering 'all the comforts of a well-regulated home', including a library. She was eventually sold in 1910 to S. Galbraith, Glasgow, and again in 1919 to the Burntisland Shipbuilding Company, where she was renamed *Fairose* and used as an accommodation ship during the construction of their shipyard, before finally being broken up in 1922.

PHOTOGRAPH BY ROBERT H. ROBERTSON, *c.* 1900

The iron screw steamer *St Nicholas* leaving Stromness. Built in 1871 at Whiteinch, Glasgow, and registered at 727 tons, she measured 228 feet by 27 feet by 14 feet, with engines that generated 200 horsepower. The transition from sailing to steam ships is clearly evident by her clipper-style bow. For over forty years, along with the first *St Clair*, she operated a regular service, mainly up and down the east coast, from Leith and Aberdeen to Orkney and Shetland, calling variously at Stromness and Kirkwall. On 17 June 1914 she ran aground on a ledge on the Proudfoot Rocks at the entrance to Wick Harbour and though she did not appear to be badly damaged, she sank the following morning. All passengers and crew were rescued by lifeboats and a local drifter.

PHOTOGRAPH BY ROBERT H. ROBERTSON, *c.* 1900

At 5 a.m. on 10 October 1920, in heavy seas, the Aberdeen trawler *Ben Namur* struck rocks in the Bay of Skaill, Sandwick, on the main island. On impact the mate and a deckhand were thrown overboard and drowned. The alarm was raised and with the help of residents in the area, the remainder of the crew succeeded in reaching the shore by deploying a rope and a wooden barrel, each in turn risking life and limb during the hazardous journey through breaking waves and dangerous rocks. Captain William Coats remained with his ship until life-saving apparatus arrived from Stromness. When she ran ashore, the *Ben Namur*, only one year old, was on her return trip from the fishing grounds with 30 tons of fish aboard. Only 4 tons of fish were retrieved and sold to local curers and though the trawler eventually became a total wreck, the boiler and engine were salvaged and refitted in another trawler by D. Grove of Aberdeen.

PHOTOGRAPH BY TOM KENT, 1920

An illustration of the physical hardship undergone by men working on roads in the early part of the twentieth century. Stone-breaking was a time-consuming procedure. The bottoming or rough stone, as it had been blasted from a local quarry, was too coarse for a finished surface and therefore 'knappers' were employed to break some of it down by the simple process of striking individual stones with a 'knapping' hammer. This finer material was then spread on top and finally dressed with a mixture of sand and clay, known as water-bound Macadam. Knappers were paid on a piece-work basis, so much per cubic yard, and they normally worked in a seated position with a cushion of sorts to give some degree of comfort. Here they are working on Old Scapa Road on the main island, near the bend towards Orphir.

PHOTOGRAPH BY TOM KENT, *c.* 1900

The arrival of the stone-crusher, driven by a
mobile steam engine through a belt-and-pulley
system, greatly relieved the arduous manual
labour involved in road-surfacing. The screens on
the crusher allowed for two different grades of
material to pass through, both of which, in this
instance, are being collected in the same cart. The
water cart on the right was for topping up the
boiler. This equipment was in use at a quarry in
Dounby on the main island.

PHOTOGRAPH BY TOM KENT, *c.* 1920

A further progression in road-making technique
shows the new steam-powered road roller bought
by the Orkney County Council. Towed behind it
were the workmen's living quarters since it was
not always possible for them to get home each
night. Following the hut came the water cart used
for spraying water on the road to help bind the
surface material.

PHOTOGRAPH BY TOM KENT, *c.* 1922

Orkney's first motorcar, a Daimler, in Harbour Street, Kirkwall. It arrived in Stromness on the *St Nicholas* in March 1901. It had been fitted out to carry eight passengers and this trial run to and around Kirkwall caused much excitement. The local press commented that it was 'much impressed, not only with its speed of 14 m.p.h. maximum, but with the clever way in which it was manoeuvred, turning corners as if on a pivot and gliding past vehicles' – presumably horse-drawn. However, the press also expressed disappointment at the number of breakdowns.

With a second vehicle already ordered, a company was formed for the purpose of running a motor service in Orkney, between Kirkwall and Stromness, with intermediate stops. It was expected that the 14-mile journey would take about one and a half hours, or half the time taken by horse coach, and that the fare was to be around half the existing charge. This company was to be known as the Orkney Express.

PHOTOGRAPH BY TOM KENT, 1901

A spectacular array of early motorised vehicles in Orkney, with some of the distinguished gentlemen who were able to afford them, assembled outside William Reid Tullock's Cycle & Motor Depot in Kirkwall in 1905. From the left: registration number s-487 is a Sterling bus, driven by Thomas Leslie, with passenger Police Constable Robert Wood; next to it is s-157, a Peugeot, built in 1904, driven by E.J. Robertson Grant of the Castle Hotel, with passenger Thomas A. Lawrie of Hobbister and standing at the back William MacLennan of Grainbank House and James Grant of Rosebank, one of the family who then owned Highland Park Distillery; a Durkopp bus, s-534, driven by William Reid Tullock himself, with passenger Charles M. Haydon, one-time owner of Lynnfield House, now a hotel, and also associated with Highland Park Distillery; a Daimler Waggonette, BS-32, driven by John Leslie, jun., with passenger Walter G. Grant, also one of the distillery owners, who lived at the time in Rosebank and later at Hillhead, both on the outskirts of Kirkwall; and finally, another Sterling bus, s-486, driven by William Leslie, brother of John, and joint owner of an engineering business in Kirkwall.

The novelty and prestige of owning and driving one of these vehicles, allied to the style and individual character of their design, must have gone a long way to compensate for solid tyres, rough roads and lack of springing.

PHOTOGRAPH BY TOM KENT, 1905

A bus outing on the main Kirkwall–Stromness road, which passed through what is now Hatston Industrial Estate. This Sterling bus belonged to E.J. Robertson Grant, the driver, and was part of the Orkney Express coach and car services, which he established in Junction Road, Kirkwall. The woman next to the driver is believed to be Mrs Haydon, daughter of James Grant, one of the family who owned Highland Park Distillery.

The large building in the background is the Ayre Mills, a grain mill which was powered by a tidal wheel.

PHOTOGRAPH BY TOM KENT, 1905

In the 1920s the decision was made to replace the Highland Park Distillery horse-drawn lorries with motorised vehicles and here are two of their lorries carting coal, used to fire the stills and kiln. In the foreground, registration number GA-676, is a petrol-driven Albion; the other vehicle is a steam-driven Sentinel.

The distillery is the largest that has ever been in Orkney. It was first operated in 1798 by David Robertson, passing through many hands, including a minister of the United Presbyterian Church and the Catholic Bishop of Aberdeen, before becoming part of the Matthew Gloag & Son Limited group of distilleries.

PHOTOGRAPH BY TOM KENT, c. 1925

The first scheduled air service to Orkney from Inverness and Wick on the Scottish mainland began on 8 May 1933 under the name Highland Airways, with the first air-mail services in Britain following the same route one year later. The inaugural flight took about fifty minutes from Inverness to Wick and a further twenty-five minutes to Kirkwall, and on board were three passengers and a consignment of the *Scotsman*

newspaper. The return flight was made later that day. The pioneer of this service was Captain Ernest Edmund Fresson OBE. He had looked into the possibility during earlier flights, firstly in April 1931 and again in February 1932 when this photograph was taken. With Captain Fresson are Heloise Pauer, his sponsor at the time and owner of the plane, John G. Shearer at the tail and David Laughton, who owned the blacksmith's shop

next door, at the propeller. Owing to threatened high winds, the plane, a de Havilland Gypsy Moth, had to be manhandled into the centre of Kirkwall and stored overnight in John G. Shearer's coal store in West Castle Street.

PHOTOGRAPH BY TOM KENT, 1932

A SENSE OF OCCASION

ORCADIANS HAVE NEVER BEEN OVERLY IMPRESSED with pomp and ceremony but they have always enjoyed a sense of occasion. Over the years they have had countless opportunities to indulge this need to kick over the traces, a need probably fostered by the drudgery of their everyday existence. Coronations, jubilees, visiting warships or dignitaries all brought them out in their hundreds, dressed in their finest clothes or, if the occasion demanded it, in fancy dress. Spasmodic events like these were punctuated by regular features such as the Lammas Market or the annual Ba' games and if all else failed, the Volunteers would organise a parade. Everyone endeavoured to take part, either as a participant or as a spectator, and any dances or other celebrations that followed the main event were avidly supported well into the early hours.

The volunteer movement in Orkney began when Thomas Balfour of Elwick on the island of Shapinsay set up his Fencibles in 1793. However, they only lasted four years and apart from a few references to a small group known as the Kirkwall Volunteer Gunners in 1801, there is no record of further development until 1860 when the Kirkwall Corps of Artillery Volunteers was formed and set up headquarters at Cromwell's Fort at the Mount on the north side of town. Other companies followed, Stromness and Sanday in 1862, Shapinsay in 1863, until each parish and island had its own small 'army' and in 1880 they collectively came to be known as the 1st Orkney Artillery Volunteers. On 10 March 1863 a gun detachment of the Kirkwall Company of the Orkney Volunteer Artillery fired the first ever official royal salute in Orkney on the occasion of the future King Edward VII's marriage. The event took place at the fort and traditional civilian wear at the time appears to have included tall hats for men and mutches for women.

PHOTOGRAPHER UNKNOWN, 1863, COPIED BY TOM KENT

On 22 June 1897 Queen Victoria's Diamond Jubilee was celebrated throughout Orkney. In Kirkwall the Royal Burgh was 'bedecked from end to end'; even boats in the harbour were decorated with flags and bunting. A grand procession was organised, led by the Artillery Band and including Kirkwall Town Council and magistrates, the two companies of the 1st Orkney Artillery Volunteers, resplendent in their uniforms, the Freemasons, the Good Templars,

the Society of Oddfellows, many of the incorporated trades of the town, such as tailors, bakers, cabinet makers, blacksmiths and yachtsmen, followed by the local school children. Tableaux, assembled on horse-drawn lorries, were a feature of the parade. They proceeded through the streets of Kirkwall, finishing at the Mount on the outskirts of town, where a twenty-one-gun salute was fired to mark the occasion. A banquet, which had been prepared

for the magistrates, members of the Town Council and 'a few gentlemen', was followed in the afternoon by a cycle run by thirty members of the Kirkwall Cycling Club, from Kirkwall to Dounby and back – a distance of some 28 miles – each participant ornamented with ribbons and flowers.

PHOTOGRAPH BY TOM KENT, 1897

Proclamations in Kirkwall are traditionally made from the market cross in front of St Magnus Cathedral. This occasion seems to have been the 'drumming in' of the Lammas Market and has attracted the usual following of local children. Making the proclamation is Bob Cumming, caretaker of the Town Hall, and the drummer supporting him is 'Dod' Harrold.

PHOTOGRAPH BY TOM KENT, *c.* 1910

It is believed the Lammas Market has taken place in Kirkwall since the Royal Charter of 1486. Its duration dropped from two weeks to three days and finally, to the first Tuesday in August, though the practice of celebrating the last, or the second, Saturday was continued for a time as well. It was the main event of the year for most Orcadians and they came from far and wide by boat, by horse transport or on foot. Open and closed stands offered a wide variety of merchandise and entertainment was provided by sideshows, street musicians and cheap-jacks, giving the occasion a carnival flavour. Though there was a livestock market held on the Broad Sands, the fair proper took place on the Kirk Green in front of St Magnus Cathedral. This was later transferred to the market 'stance' or grounds at Walliwall on the outskirts of town, before giving way, eventually, to the annual County Show held at Bignold Park in Kirkwall. It has recently been revived as the St Magnus Fair, a fund-raising occasion for the conservation of St Magnus Cathedral, returning to its original site on Broad Street. Records show that revelry was inclined to get out of hand and a Lammas guard was appointed to keep the peace, from the small standing army that existed in Kirkwall at the time. In 1732, they had occasion to deal with about forty young men, mostly from Caithness and Sutherland on the Scottish mainland, who turned up armed with swords and pistols. The term 'Lammas bed' referred to the floors of empty houses, where young persons of both sexes bedded down free of charge, during the time of the fair. Inevitably many permanent relationships developed from the event.

PHOTOGRAPH BY TOM KENT, *c.* 1900

On 22 June 1911 Coronation Day celebrations for George V were held throughout Orkney. In Kirkwall they began in the morning with a service in St Magnus Cathedral. This was followed by a procession through the town by the magistrates and members of Kirkwall Town Council supported by various local societies and organisations, and led by the Territorial Band. The Orkney Royal Garrison Artillery (Territorial), the Freemasons, the Good Templars, the Rechabites and the Boys' Brigade turned out in force to give a memorable display. From the market cross, an address was given by Provost James Slater and to mark the occasion some 120 poor people in the town received gifts of money.

In the evening a fancy-dress cycle parade, supported by almost a hundred cyclists, assembled outside the skating rink, now the Casablanca Disco. They paraded to Broad Street, where judging took place, before proceeding through the town. The final event of the day was a dance sponsored by Kirkwall Town Council in the Town Hall.

PHOTOGRAPH BY TOM KENT, 1911

During the summer, on less formal occasions, spare time was occupied in leisure pursuits, either actively in sports or games or in a more relaxed mood in the form of a picnic, usually at the shore. They may have been organised by the church, the school, the parish council or by societies like the Good Templars or Freemasons or they may simply have been family affairs. Each parish or island held its official annual sports meeting, normally as part of the agricultural show. Inter-district competitions were also popular and great rivalry was engendered by the raucous, but malice-free, taunts of 'Scooties', 'Limpets', 'Bloody-puddings' or whatever was the appropriate district name for those involved. Such events invariably ended with a set meal and a dance, where all the day's rivalry was forgotten and old and new friendships fostered in an atmosphere of mutual regard.

Games, whether at a picnic or at home, usually involved everyone, with grandad, willingly or not, as much a part of the revelry as the youngest child and such favourites as 'hide-and-seek' or 'offers-and-catchers' passed many a happy hour. Food also played an important part in the picnic. Baskets were carefully packed with home-baked bread, biscuits, cheese, milk, lemonade and so on – something for everyone and ample to satisfy even the most voracious appetite. A small open fire was built from beach stones to heat water for the tea. Emergencies were taken in their stride – hankies were tied round skinned knees and cut fingers, nettle stings were treated with dock

leaves, bumped heads were mended with a kiss and a dab of butter, and wet clothes were spread out on the rocks to dry in the sun.

There were clamours of protest when home time was announced, but there were cows to be milked and hens to be fed and without further ado, each picked up his or her share of the load and made for home on foot, on bicycle or, if you were lucky, in a cart or gig. A convoy of picnickers (opposite) are heading for the beach at Skaill, passing Skaill Loch in the main-island

parish of Sandwick. The family group (above) are thoroughly enjoying their refreshments, especially the young man with the bottle to his head, although the minister looks less than merry.

PHOTOGRAPHS: ABOVE BY DAVID HORNE, *c*. 1920; OPPOSITE BY ROBERT H. ROBERTSON, *c*. 1900

This may appear to some as an unruly mob but it is in fact one of Orkney's longest-standing traditions. Played through the streets of Kirkwall on Christmas Day and New Year's Day, it is known as 'The Ba''. Its origins are unknown but it resembles other mass football games played elsewhere in Britain. The contestants are divided into two huge teams – 'Up-the-gates' and 'Down-the-gates' or better known locally as 'Uppies' and 'Doonies'. Basically, the division is decided by place of birth but since most children are now born in one hospital, it is by the home in which their parents live at the time of the birth. The dividing line runs from east to west through the starting point in the centre of town, the market cross. Non-Orcadians living in Orkney

are expected to play according to where they first arrived, that is, north or south of the dividing line and this is dictated mainly by whether they arrived by aeroplane or boat.

No set rules are laid down for the Ba' but certain conventions and a degree of etiquette apply to raise it above the level of a free-for-all. Tactics are also very much a part of the play and techniques such as 'rolling' or 'smuggling' are well understood by the participants. The object of the game is for the Doonies to get the ba' or ball down and into the harbour, while the Uppies strive to take it up the street to a fixed point still known variously as Mackinson's Corner, Sandison's Corner or the Long Corner, which must be touched by the ba'. It is played in the

morning by young boys and in the afternoon by men.

There was also a Youths' Ba' played for many years by teenage boys and an experiment with a Ladies' Ba' on Christmas Day 1945 and New Year's Day 1946, which to say was undignified would hardly do justice to the passions, ferocity and whatever else was displayed on that disastrous occasion. The experiment has never been repeated. This is the New Year's Day Men's Ba' of 1911, still on Broad Street, which was won by Jack Scollay, adjudged by the majority of his team to have played longest and hardest over the years.

PHOTOGRAPH BY TOM KENT, 1911

OUR ANCIENT HERITAGE

ORKNEY HAS A WEALTH OF ARCHAEOLOGICAL REMAINS. It offers a range of important monuments and sites, contained in a relatively small area, un-equalled anywhere in Britain. Though people had been aware of their existence for many centuries, with monuments such as the Ring of Brodgar, Orkney's 'Stone-henge', there for all to see, they were often looked upon with a good measure of suspicion as places of religious or supernatural significance. It was only in the mid-nineteenth century that serious excavation and examination began. Locals took an active interest in early digs and some very good excavation and recording work was done but it was probably the visits of the eminent archaeologist James Farrer that started a period of feverish antiquarian activity. On the main island he examined the newly uncovered ruins at Skara Brae in 1855 and later began his excavation of the chambered tomb at Maeshowe in 1861. Several notable Orcadians, in particular James W. Cursiter, became involved. They joined, and submitted papers to, the Society of Antiquaries of Scotland and later in 1922 formed the Orkney Record and Antiquarian Society. This interest has not waned over the years and recently a full-time archaeologist has been appointed to control all excavation work now being undertaken in Orkney. The written records of these sites were left to the archaeologists concerned, but the pictorial recording was done by local photographers of the calibre of Tom Kent, fortunately available at a time of great activity.

Skara Brae in the parish of Sandwick on the main island is a prehistoric settlement which was founded some 5,000 years ago. It is believed to have been inhabited for a period of about 600 years and offered accommodation for about fifty people. Uncovered by a storm in 1850, it was originally given a thorough examination between 1855 and 1860 by James Farrer. Further studies were made between 1860 and 1867 by William W.G. Watt, the owner of the land on which it stood, and in 1913 by Balfour Stewart but it was in 1927, under the auspices of the Office of Works, that Professor V. Gordon Childe began the detailed and extensive restoration we see today. What remains consists of six subterranean houses, linked together by passages, and one 'outhouse', probably a workshop. Each house has a strong resemblance to the one next door, offering spacious accommodation with storage and lavatory areas recessed into the walls. The remains of the interior furnishings are in an excellent state of preservation.

PHOTOGRAPH BY TOM KENT, *c.* 1930

This strange object, known as the Dwarfie Stone, lies close to the Rackwick Road on the island of Hoy and has attracted many photographers over the years. Carved with stone tools from a solid block of sandstone, inside there is a small chamber with two side cells. Nearby lies a large stone, originally used for blocking the entrance. It is 28 feet long, 14 feet 8 inches wide at one end and 13 feet at the other, and is 6 feet 8 inches high at one end and 3 feet at the other. The entrance is 2 feet 4 inches high and 2 feet 10 inches wide. It is believed to have been a tomb but nothing is known of what became of its contents.

PHOTOGRAPH BY TOM KENT, *c.* 1900

Henge monuments in Orkney are numerous. In this particular area at Brodgar in Stenness on the main island there are the remains of two circles – the Stones of Stenness depicted in the foreground and the much larger and more famous Ring of Brodgar in the distance on the far left. The Stones of Stenness are believed to date from the third millennium BC. Originally, the circle would have consisted of twelve slabs in a circle almost 98½ feet in diameter but only four of the originals remain. It was surrounded by a ditch approximately 23 feet wide and 6½ feet deep, hewn from solid rock. The Ring of Brodgar is considered by many to be even more spectacular than Stonehenge. Dating from the same period as the Stones of Stenness, it originally consisted of some sixty slabs, in a perfect circle, twenty-seven of which remain standing, and has a diameter of approximately 341 feet. The ditch surrounding it was almost 33 feet wide with two entrances. The stones vary in height from 6½ feet to 14½ feet. Though considered to have some religious or ceremonial significance, their existence remains something of a mystery. The Watchstone, a magnificent monolith standing 18 feet high, rises on its own between the causeway and the edge of Stenness Loch. It can be seen on the right of the picture.

PHOTOGRAPH BY TOM KENT, c. 1900

This dovecote at the Hall of Rendall, in the main-island parish of Rendall, is unique in Orkney. Nests were arranged for the pigeons by leaving irregular gaps in the internal stonework. It dates from the seventeenth century and still remains in good structural condition.

PHOTOGRAPH BY TOM KENT, *c.* 1900

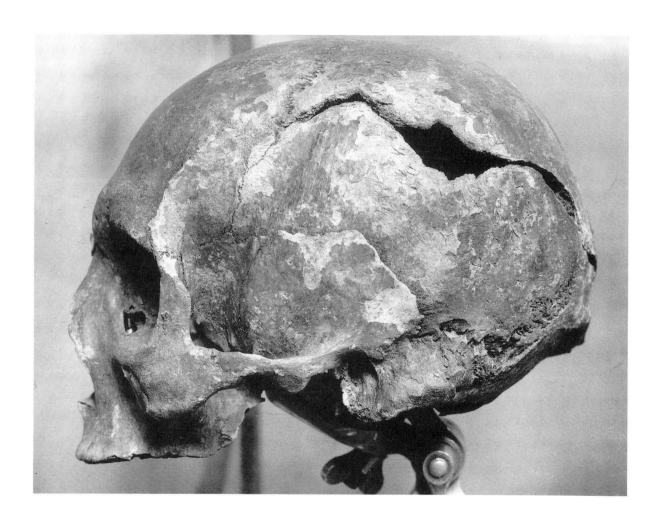

The skull of St Magnus, Earl of Orkney, photographed in 1925 after its exhumation. It was discovered with other remains in a casket in one of the pillars of St Magnus Cathedral during restoration work. A thorough examination by Sir R.W. Reid, Emeritus Professor of Anatomy at Aberdeen University, revealed clear evidence of the blow which killed him, as related in the sagas. St Magnus had been Earl of Orkney from about 1106 to 1116, a position he held jointly with his cousin Hakon. Bad blood existed between them and a conference was arranged on the small island of Egilsay, with the intention of improving their relationship. However, the treacherous Hakon arrived that Easter Day with eight ships full of armed men instead of the two that had been agreed. He took Magnus prisoner and ordered his reluctant cook Lifolf to strike the fatal blow with an axe. He was first buried in Christchurch in Birsay, then taken to St Olaf's Church in Kirkwall, before reaching his final resting place in St Magnus Cathedral. The cathedral was erected in his memory by his nephew St Rognvald, who also became Earl of Orkney 1156–8.

PHOTOGRAPH BY TOM KENT, 1925

The Broch of Gurness at Aikerness in Evie on the main island is one of many broch sites in Orkney of which at least fifty-two are identifiable. Its particular importance is that it is considered to have the most extensive and well-preserved domestic buildings, outside the broch itself, to be found in Scotland. Though evidently brochs were basically defensive in structure, dating from somewhere between the first century BC and the ninth century AD, they are still something of a mystery in spite of having been tackled by many of the foremost archaeological minds in the country. Originally in the form of a tall tower with hollow walls, Gurness was much reduced in height when this photograph was taken during excavation work in 1930. Seen clearly are the rectangular hearth, the steps leading down to the well and some of the internal furnishings.

PHOTOGRAPH BY TOM KENT, 1930

147

WHAT WE BUILT

BUILDING IS A BROAD SUBJECT and its development in Orkney, particularly with reference to houses, is excellently described in Alexander Fenton's book *The Northern Isles*. Our houses vary enormously, from the traditional longhouse to the splendid mansions, palaces or castles that are scattered throughout the islands. The contrasts are evocative, particularly in communities such as the island of Rousay, where the laird was something less than a benefactor and long memories may yet recall the 'big house' as a symbol of much of the hardships our forefathers had to endure.

The most outstanding building in the islands is St Magnus Cathedral, Kirkwall, which celebrated its 850th anniversary in 1987. The splendour of its design, externally and internally, constructed throughout in local red sandstone, has inspired many writers, artists and photographers in Orkney and from elsewhere. Though it was built during the Norse occupation of Orkney, there is nothing Norse in its design nor in the method of its building, most of the work being carried out by masons of the Durham school. It is considered to be one of the two finest and most complete cathedral churches in Scotland – the other being Glasgow Cathedral.

Building materials have always been dictated by availability, cost and climate. Little timber is grown here and therefore driftwood, plentiful in some islands in years past, has been heavily supplemented by imported supplies. Stone has always been preferred to brick since it is widely available and even now when it has become too expensive to dress and build in the traditional way, it is crushed and made into concrete blocks which can be erected quickly like bricks. Roofing was mainly straw or flagstones, both locally produced.

In addition to houses and the cathedral, photographers have recorded the full range of what we built – shops, churches, schools, hospitals and so on – and what is equally important, they often had the foresight to take photographs of what these buildings replaced.

St Magnus Cathedral was erected at the wish of St Rognvald, Earl of Orkney, in memory of his murdered uncle, St Magnus, to a plan of Rognvald's father, Kol. Begun in 1137, it has been extended and extensively altered on several occasions. But only since Sheriff George Thoms, who held office here from 1890 to 1899, left the generous sum of £60,000 in the hands of Kirkwall magistrates specifically for the restoration and upkeep of the cathedral, has it been properly cared for.

Prior to the extensive restoration work carried out under the Thoms's Trust, this view shows the short spire and the open turret below, which were replaced by the present tall spire and enclosed tower, complete with gargoyles and new clock. New dykes were also put around the churchyard. A recent addition is the installation of a stained-glass window to commemorate the 850th anniversary of the cathedral in 1987.

PHOTOGRAPH BY GEORGE W. WILSON, *c.* 1890

St Magnus Cathedral has housed
Catholics, Episcopalians and
Presbyterians to comply with what
prevailed at the time and today it is
Church of Scotland. Maintenance
throughout the centuries has been a
haphazard affair and often the church
has suffered appallingly from neglect.
It was damaged during Cromwell's
siege in 1651 and suffered for a time
when it acted as a barracks for the
Roundheads, including their horses; it
was struck by lightning in 1671,
destroying the steeple and much of the
interior timber in its vicinity; and in
general it was badly misused.
As a result of the Thoms's Trust,
restoration work was carried out
between 1913 and 1930 under the
guidance of Edinburgh architect
George Mackie Watson. The screens
enclosing the choir were removed; the
nineteenth-century pews and
galleries, reserved for the use of the
landed gentry, were torn out; the old
pulpit, seen here, was replaced; a
taller, copper-clad spire was erected in
place of the short stone pyramid that
existed; the floor was restored to its
original level and flagstones gave way
to coloured tiles; stained glass was
fitted to most of the windows; new
lighting was put in; the Communion
table and choir stalls were renewed;
and a large new pipe organ was
installed. It was a magnificent effort,
befitting an edifice of such stature.
Since that time regular maintenance
has continued and is now the
responsibility of the Orkney Islands
Council in conjunction with the
Society of Friends of St Magnus,
formed in 1958, and the Appeal
Committee, which came into being in
1971 when further expensive repairs
became urgent. An event which they
organise annually to raise money is the
St Magnus Fair, a mock version of the
old Lammas Market, which
traditionally had been held for many
centuries on the Kirk Green. All
attempts to take over responsibility

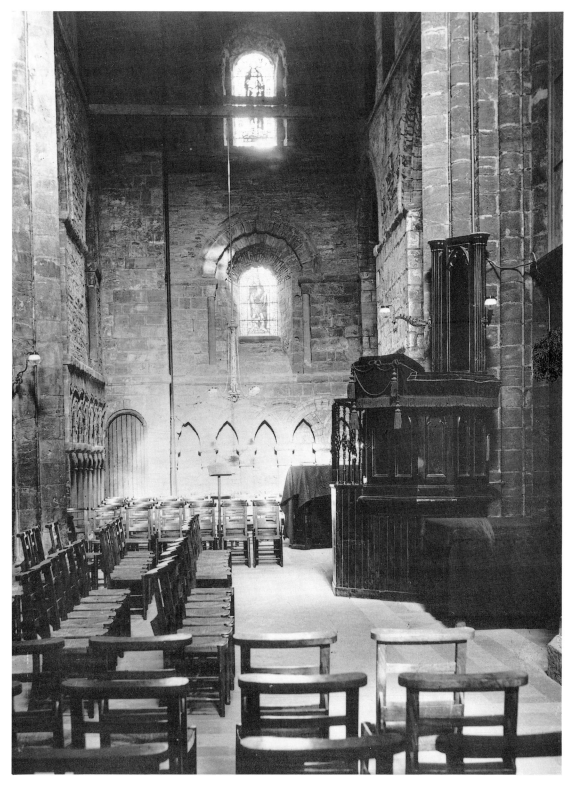

for the cathedral's upkeep by the Ministry of
Works and its successor the Department of the
Environment have been so far resisted in a bid to
avoid restrictions which would be imposed if the
cathedral were to be listed as a national
monument instead of a living church. The
photograph above depicts the nave.

PHOTOGRAPHS: ABOVE BY GEORGE W. WILSON,
c. 1890; OPPOSITE BY TOM KENT, *c.* 1905

Kirkwall Grammar School was first built on this site in 1820. It had been in existence for over 400 years prior to this, housed in various buildings mostly attached to St Magnus Cathedral and for a time in the cathedral itself. Early teachers were churchmen and the first full-time schoolmaster, believed to be Thomas Houston, who resigned in 1595, was appointed in 1544 by Bishop Reid. The building was erected on ground offered by Samuel Laing of Papdale, outside Kirkwall, by James Allan, contractor, from plans prepared by Mr Gillespie, architect. Originally designed for 150 boys, it became 'mixed' when, as a result of the 1872 Education Act, the Infant School and Subscription School in Kirkwall were amalgamated with it.

Kirkwall Grammar School's first headmaster was David Paterson, a tall raw-boned man with a reputation for being something of a tyrant. However, his reign was short, as he deserted his post in October 1822 and went south. Probably its most distinguished head was Dr John McEwan, rector from 1879 to 1914, and under whose control the number of pupils rose from 60 to 600. A number of eminent scholars have been produced by the school, among them poet and literary critic Edwin Muir; Dr Stanley Cursiter, artist and Keeper of the National Galleries of Scotland; William Balfour Baikie, explorer of the River Niger; the engraver Sir Robert Strange; Thomas S. Clouston, pioneer in psychiatric medicine; Hugh Marwick, authority on the Norn language; and Sir James D.

Marwick, town clerk of both Edinburgh and Glasgow during his distinguished career in local government. By 1900, after extensive alterations and renovations, the building had undergone the transformation shown above, before being recently converted into new offices for the Orkney Islands Council. It has been replaced by a modern secondary, two primaries and an infant school on other sites in the town.

Though not in school uniform, the children above were a good deal more formally dressed than is the case now. Other noticeable features are the number of cart tracks on the clay road surface and the complete absence of the motorcar.

PHOTOGRAPHS: OPPOSITE BY UNKNOWN PHOTOGRAPHER, *c.* 1860; ABOVE BY TOM KENT, *c.* 1900

The original part of Stromness Academy was
built in 1870. By 1903 the need for expansion
was recognised, particularly for a new higher
grade school, and plans were prepared at the
request of the School Board by William
Robertson, architect. A tender of £1,757,
submitted by builder Alexander Guthrie, was
accepted, the work to be finished within twelve
months of signing the contract. Classes moved
into the new premises on 3 November 1905,
though the school logbook records that 'the gas
pipes have not yet been brought within 200 yards
of the building'. In other respects the rooms were
adjudged to be 'very comfortable'. This building
has now been vacated in favour of a modern new
secondary school complex at Garson on the
north end of town and the fate of the old school is
still under review. This photograph, clearly posed
for, was taken during the 1904–5 extension and
illustrates a number of old carpenters' tools: the
two-handed saw; the wooden planes; the hand
brace; and the drawknife. Quality materials were
used in the construction, most of the timber being
Oregon or pitch pine.

PHOTOGRAPH BY ROBERT H. ROBERTSON, *c.* 1904

The old Balfour Hospital in Main Street, Kirkwall, the first hospital in Orkney, was opened in 1845. John Balfour of Trenaby on the island of Westray had long since recognised the need for proper medical care in Orkney and in 1836 he placed £20,000 of Mexican Bonds in the hands of trustees, appointed to act on his behalf. These bonds realised the princely sum of £6,049.8s.1d., which was invested on heritable security until 1845. The building became known as the Orkney Hospital and in 1853 it was renamed the Orkney Balfour Hospital and finally abbreviated to the Balfour Hospital. Originally a private house, bought from merchant James

Shearer, Kirkwall, for £450, the building soon proved to be too small and other adjacent properties were added, before the new fever hospital was built, behind and to the right. This great asset was intended mainly for the poor and the hospital's first regulation states 'That a preference be given to destitute patients labouring under fever or contagious or acute disease, or requiring surgical treatment.' In the late nineteenth century scarlet fever, tuberculosis, diphtheria and smallpox were regular health hazards in Orkney and in 1878 fifty patients are recorded in the ordinary ward and twenty-two in the fever ward. When it became clear that the

building was no longer suitable a new hospital was planned and in 1926, after several years' delay, the new Garden Memorial Building, donated by the widow of Robert Garden, was built on the south side of town. The official name has long since disappeared, Orcadians having faithfully reverted to the old name, and the Balfour Hospital remains as the medical centre for the islands. The original building, photographed here on a winter's day, is now the West End Hotel.

PHOTOGRAPH BY TOM KENT, *c. 1900*

Orkney was subject to many serious diseases, some contagious, but none worse than tuberculosis. A combination of bad living conditions, in particular damp housing, and the prevalence of milk from non-attested cattle made it one of the main 'killer' diseases throughout the islands. So common was it that few families were not touched by it and along with scarlet fever, diphtheria and smallpox it was accepted as a normal hazard of life. Though not highly contagious, tuberculosis could be passed on and for this reason a certain degree of isolation was considered desirable. This factor, combined with

the only known medium for alleviating the condition, fresh air, prompted the Health Board to look for a suitable site for a TB hospital and the vacant Scapa Seaplane Base came under consideration. After prolonged negotiations with the admiralty between 1920 and 1923, the huts were bought and a tender for their conversion submitted by Samuel Baikie & Son, Kirkwall, was accepted. What came to be known as the Scapa Tuberculosis Pavilion was opened in 1924, providing accommodation for twelve patients. It was extended and a laundry added later. The verandah played an important role in the

patients' care and whenever the weather was reasonable they were taken outside to get what benefit they could from the fresh sea air. However, the life of the Scapa Pavilion was short as the need for more accommodation became urgent and a new custom-built Tuberculosis and Infectious Diseases Hospital was built at Eastbank on the outskirts of Kirkwall and opened in 1937.

PHOTOGRAPH BY TOM KENT, c. 1930

After the disruption of 1843, when the established Church of Scotland split into various churches, three emerged on the island of Sanday: the Free Church, the United Presbyterian Church, and the traditional Church of Scotland. During the religious revivals of the 1860s, congregations grew and many new churches were built. Revd John Paul, United Presbyterian minister in Sanday for many years, along with his assistant Revd David Calderwood, was held in very high regard and the congregation increased greatly. By 1879 the membership had risen to 566, with 5 sabbath schools, 39 teachers and 220 scholars scattered throughout the island. As the church

was financially sound, it was decided to build a new church to replace the existing one, which had become inadequate and unsafe. Architect Samuel Baikie, Kirkwall, and builder William Robertson, Stromness (believed to be the gentleman conversing in the foreground on the right), were entrusted to provide a new building that was 'substantial, and well ventilated, and at a cost of not more than £2 per sitting' to cater for a congregation of 800. Revd Calderwood and his congregation were offered accommodation in the Free Church by the Revd Matthew Armour while the new building was under construction. In the event the original estimate was exceeded by

about £500 and the church went into debt, £500 to the Synod and a further £500 to a private source, which was only finally cleared by 1896.

At least nine of the large work force are occupied in dressing the sandstone blocks with chisels and wooden mallets and a further eleven, up on the scaffold, are doing the actual building, helped by several labourers and foremen on the ground. The new United Presbyterian Church was completed in 1882.

PHOTOGRAPH BY UNKNOWN PHOTOGRAPHER, 1881

The old Town Hall or Tolbooth in Kirkwall, which stood in front of St Magnus Cathedral at the southern end of Kirk Green, was built at the wishes of Lord Morton, Earl of Orkney. For this purpose, he donated £200 from damages received from Sir James Stewart of the island of Burray, who was found guilty of discharging a musket at a boat containing the said earl, while crossing Holm Sound with a prisoner from the Stewart household. He expressed the view that the existing prison was out of date and that 'prisoners could not be securely warded without appearance of hardship or cruelty'. The new building was completed in 1740 and served as Town Hall, prison, courtroom, guardhouse, and Masonic Lodge. A small room, leading off from the courtroom, housed the public library for a time.

Much of Kirkwall's social history centred around the Tolbooth. Great banquets and balls were held in the assembly room. The Orcadian

writer James Fea describes the gathering of ladies 'brilliant as to figure, education, virtue and every other amiable qualification' and 'gentlemen in scarlet vests and top boots' devouring heavy suppers with 'rounds of boiled beef smothered in cabbage, smoked geese, mutton hams, roasts of pork, dishes of dog fish and Welsh rabbits, and washed down with strong home-brewed ale and large bowls of rum punch'. Whist and brag were also played and stakes often ran high.

Immediately below, however, where sanitary conditions and security left a lot to be desired, all sorts of skulduggery took place. Spirits, gingerbread and other prohibited goods were regularly slipped in through windows to the inmates and several escapes were effected. Jailors were poorly paid and varied greatly in their application to their work. Some were scorned for their carelessness, while others enjoyed a reputation for brutality. In 1827 one woman prisoner hanged herself from a cord passed in

through her window. Earmarked for the gallows anyway for poisoning her husband, the taunts and jeers of people outside drove her to take her own life. Sheriff James A. MacConochie remarked at the time that 'the jail is a disgrace to the county; it is neither fit for confinement with security, nor as a place of punishment to the guilty; and the jailor is nearly as good as the jail, for he did not visit his charge the day after the woman had strangled herself till one o'clock afternoon'. The need for the old Tolbooth disappeared with the building of the new County Buildings and Court Room in 1877, the new Town Hall in 1886 and the new Masonic Lodge in 1887 and mercifully, after a long life of 150 years, this blight on the landscape at last was removed.

PHOTOGRAPH BY GEORGE W. WILSON, c. 1890

Although he had been laird of the island of Rousay since 1847, Lieutenant General Frederick W. Traill Burroughs only came to live in Orkney in 1870. It was an event that was to be deeply etched in the memories of the inhabitants for many years. Small and bearded, he limped ashore, suffering from a wound received at the Battle of Lucknow, during the Indian Mutiny, and was given a warm welcome by his tenants. Lucknow was not to be his last battle as he began systematically clearing out the crofters by rack-renting and evictions. However, he reckoned without the resilience of some of his tenants and

many serious confrontations took place, some violent, before the intervention of a gunboat, sent to put down a riot, and a special Act of Parliament was rushed through to curb his tyranny. The Napier Commission of 1883, leading to the Crofters Act of 1886, finally put a stop to his campaign of oppression but not before untold damage had been inflicted on the community. From a historical point of view, one of his more serious crimes was to put to the torch most of the official records concerning Rousay. Trumland House was his home. It was built in 1872–3 from plans drawn by David Bryce of Edinburgh,

architect of Balfour Castle, Berstane House and Kirkwall Sheriff Court. Built in the Jacobean style it was finished to a very high standard and furnished as befitted a person of some standing. It also sported one of the few woodland areas in Orkney, where peacocks roamed at will. In 1985 a serious fire destroyed a great deal of the beautiful interior woodwork and restoration work is still in progress.

PHOTOGRAPH BY TOM KENT, 1930

Graemeshall stands near the village of St Mary's in the main-island parish of Holm. The original part of the house, probably built in the fifteenth century, was the house of Meall and it was removed during extensive alterations in 1874. The earliest existing part built either by Bishop George Graeme or by his son-in-law Patrick Smyth of Braco in Perthshire, in 1626. It remained in the hands of the Graeme family up until 1960. The photograph opposite of the main entrance archway was taken just before the renovations of 1874 and the subjects almost certainly include Alexander Sutherland Graeme (1806–94), 7th Laird of Graemeshall, with his wife Mary Ann and possibly his sons Alexander Malcolm and Patrick Neale. Graemeshall was the scene of at least one violent confrontation when Sir James Stewart of the island of Burray arrived with about thirty armed men to take issue with James Douglas, Earl of Morton. It was one incident in a long feud over the unfair method by which Stewart extracted superior duties from his tenants by using inaccurate weights. Fortunately, no fatalities occurred but Stewart was fined heavily for the assault. Graemeshall is now owned by Norris Wood, who has spent a lifetime collecting antiques, and part of the building containing this fine collection is open to the public.

PHOTOGRAPHS: ABOVE BY TOM KENT, c. 1900; OPPOSITE BY UNKNOWN PHOTOGRAPHER, c. 1870

Netherby in Deerness on the main island illustrates what the interior of a typical rural house looked like around the turn of the century. The focal point was the central fireplace, which normally burned peat, and most of the smoke was expected to escape through a hole in the roof, directly above. The method of cooking is well portrayed – heavy pots or kettles suspended by a chain from the rafters. The triangular shaped object on top of the fire was the heated part of a domestic iron, which was encased in a similarly shaped cover with handle attached, and replaced as it cooled down by another at the required temperature. The 'box' beds in the background, with sliding panel doors, were a standard feature, and the mattresses would have been filled with chaff or corn husks. Other items normally found in an Orkney home were the spinning wheel, straw-backed chairs and oil lamps.

PHOTOGRAPH BY TOM KENT, *c.* 1902

Burness House is a two-storeyed dwelling in the main-island parish of Firth. Grander than most farmhouses of its day, it sported an inglenook, rare in Orkney. Again there are many items common to houses of the period – the oil lamps, including a cruisie, the meat and fish hanging to cure, the 'girnel' for meal, the food press, the plate rack, the peat 'cubbie', the heavy iron pots suspended over the fire, even a toasting fork and a melodion. The warm flagstones near the fireplace would have been much appreciated by the old collie dog after his day's work.

PHOTOGRAPH BY TOM KENT, *c.* 1900

Crofts in Orkney were, for over a thousand years, based on the early longhouse. Found elsewhere in the British Isles and in Scandinavia, there is some conjecture as to whether the longhouse came here with the Vikings or whether they brought it back with them to Norway and Denmark. The main feature of this type of dwelling, as its name implies, is that it is formed by building a number of compartments end to end in linear form. The basic sequence was byre, kitchen, scullery and room, but often additional units such as the barn were added at either end, the whole building

being linked internally by communicating doors and occasionally sharing a common exit. An alternative was to add a parallel sequence of outhouses with a narrow close in between, which is the form adopted here. The layout gave a certain 'atmosphere' and undoubtedly offered a form of shared warmth in winter. The 'simmens' roofing was a common feature of the poorer houses in Orkney. Ropes or simmens were hand made by twisting layers of heather or straw and then woven from the wall head to the one opposite, over the ridge, to form a bed. This was

overlaid with loose straw and another layer of simmens woven on top. This process was continued until the roof was considered to be 'tight' and flagstones along the eaves formed a securing point for the simmens. Other features common to crofts in Orkney were the small stackyard, the 'plantiecrue' or garden enclosure for raising kail or cabbage and, of course, the midden, the dunghill on the right. This croft was in the district of Tankerness.

PHOTOGRAPH BY TOM KENT, c. 1900

Skaill House, which stands near the prehistoric
village of Skara Brae in the main-island parish of
Sandwick, was probably built at the beginning of
the seventeenth century by Bishop George
Graeme, one of Orkney's great builders.
Considerable alterations and additions have
been effected over the years but the oldest part
is on the left.

PHOTOGRAPH BY TOM KENT, *c*. 1900

The Earl's Palace in Kirkwall was built during the first few years of the seventeenth century by the notorious Earl of Orkney, Patrick Stewart. It was handed over to Bishop James Law in 1607 and the last episcopal occupant, 1677–88, was Bishop Murdo MacKenzie. It was never fully completed but has been described as possibly the most mature and accomplished piece of Renaissance architecture left in Scotland. The great hall probably best illustrates this: at 55 feet long and 20 feet 4 inches wide it contains one very large arched fireplace on one wall and a smaller one on an adjacent wall. The large three-light window faces south, while two large bay windows face east. Hay is lying, in the foreground, on an area now occupied by Kirkwall Bowling Green. The building was extensively renovated by the Ministry of Works when it took over responsibility for its upkeep in 1920. Patrick Stewart, along with his equally tyrannous father Robert, ruled Orkney with a rod of iron for fifty years before being brought to justice and executed in Edinburgh in 1615.

PHOTOGRAPH BY GEORGE W. WILSON, *c.* 1890

The Watergate in Kirkwall, which gave its name to the present street, was removed in 1877 to widen the access for vehicles and rebuilt into the wall of the old Bishop's Palace. The palace has been reconstructed on several occasions and the layout of the original building can no longer be determined. Most of what remains was built by Bishop Robert Reid at the end of the fifteenth and the beginning of the sixteenth centuries. As well as serving as the residence of several of Orkney's many bishops, it was also the last refuge of the Norwegian King Hakon Hakonson, after his ill-fated expedition to Scotland, which ended so disastrously in 1263 at the Battle of Largs. After a few weeks of sickness he died here and was then temporarily laid to rest in St Magnus Cathedral nearby, before being taken back to Norway for burial.

This photograph was taken from the tower of the cathedral. The old house beyond the palace served for many years as accommodation for various dignitaries attached to the cathedral and though it has been a private dwelling house for a long time now, it is still called the Old Manse.

PHOTOGRAPH BY UNKNOWN PHOTOGRAPHER, c. 1870, COPIED BY TOM KENT

James Flett, a tailor by trade, returned from Canada and in 1871 began trading as a grocer and ironmonger in Bridge Street, Kirkwall. His business expanded rapidly and on the same site he built the new Anchor Buildings in 1904. A later addition was achieved in 1919 by roofing over the existing Anchor Close to form a large store, using materials from a disused seaplane station. Further expansion was made in 1934. In its heyday the firm consisted of a hardware and grocery shop, a sweet shop, a bread shop, a bakery and a seeds and manure store. It owned several boats, including the schooner *Queen of the Isles*; two smacks, the *Narcissus* and the *Mountaineer*; and a clipper used for transporting coal and other goods to and from the south. It also ran several horse-drawn vans and lorries, which were superseded by motorised vehicles and a second shop was opened in the main-island village of Finstown. It passed through four generations before it ceased trading in 1982. In January 1985 a serious fire caused much damage to the premises, particularly to the roof, but it is fully utilised once more as an arcade catering for a variety of small traders, many selling local crafts.

PHOTOGRAPH BY TOM KENT, c. 1910

BEFORE THE FIRE, STROMNESS, FEBY 18TH 1910.

R.H.R.

On 18 February 1910, at the North End of Stromness, the newly opened Farmers' Supply Stores, owned by Samuel Baikie, was totally destroyed by fire. Damage was estimated at between £8,000 and £10,000, which was only in part covered by insurance. The alarm had been raised at about 2.30 a.m. but in spite of valiant efforts by fire-fighters the store was completely gutted, even the 'fire-proof' safe proving useless against the intense heat, its entire contents being destroyed. There were fears that the fire would spread to adjacent buildings, in particular to the local gasworks which was situated almost next door, but fortunately this was averted.

PHOTOGRAPH BY ROBERT H. ROBERTSON, 1910

The gutted Farmers' Supply Stores, destroyed by
fire on 18 February 1910. The buildings were
subsequently refurbished and restocked and
there was trading for many years until recently,
when the current owners, Robert and David
Sinclair, transferred their business to larger
premises nearby. The building now operates as a
furniture shop.

PHOTOGRAPH BY TOM KENT, 1910

170

THE ANCHORAGE

ORKNEY HAD A LONG ASSOCIATION WITH THE BRITISH NAVY that lasted over 150 years. A case was first made in 1812 by the distinguished admiralty hydrographer Graeme Spence, who proposed to establish Scapa Flow as a rendezvous base for merchant shipping, awaiting naval escort. The threat of Napoleon had placed Britain's merchant fleet in jeopardy, particularly in the English Channel, and when our relations with America also began to deteriorate, the newly preferred alternative northern route to the Baltic, via the Pentland Firth, became hazardous, as our ships were attacked by American privateers off western and northern coasts. The first move to defend this assembly point at Longhope on the island of Hoy occurred in 1815, when a small eight-gun battery and two Martello towers were established. From that time Scapa Flow featured regularly in the plans and movements of naval ships. In 1912 it was officially designated a naval anchorage by the admiralty and it fulfilled this vital role through two world wars, before it was finally closed down on 29 March 1957.

Fleet visits to the Kirkwall Roads were also commonplace, particularly prior to 1912, and every summer we could expect one or several occasions when naval personnel added life and colour to our town.

The Channel Fleet's visit to Kirkwall during 15–20 July 1898 was of significance, since it had on board the Duke of York and Prince Louis of Battenberg, accompanied by Admirals Stephenson and Brackenbury. In all there were eight first-class battleships, two first-class cruisers, three second-class cruisers and one third-class cruiser. This was the largest naval assembly in Orkney up until that time and for a day Kirkwall doubled its population when 3,555 blue-jackets from six battalions, each with its own band, paraded through the town. The duke, accompanied by the other distinguished visitors, took the official salute from the market cross, at a march past in Broad Street. Part of this huge contingent is seen in the photograph, stretching along Harbour Street, Shore Street and down the main pier. During the week the customary hospitality was extended and many were entertained by local clubs and organisations.

PHOTOGRAPH BY TOM KENT, 1898

On 14 June 1899 ships of the Training Squadron, HMS *Champion*, HMS *Volage*, HMS *Cleopatra*, and the flagship HMS *Raleigh*, arrived in Kirkwall Bay. Much interest was created when the ships were opened daily to the public, a practice that continued over the years during naval visits to Orkney. Several hundred sailors were allowed ashore and competitions with local clubs, involving golf, tennis, fishing and shooting, were arranged. Two unfortunate incidents occurred during their stay. A sailor, Ashley Jones, was killed in a fall aboard HMS *Raleigh* and a local labourer, John Cassells, was drowned while sailing around the anchored warships. Ashley Jones was buried with full naval honours in the churchyard of St Magnus Cathedral.

PHOTOGRAPH BY TOM KENT, 1899

This very attractive photograph was taken in August 1906, during the visit to Kirkwall of the 1st and 2nd divisions of the Torpedo Flotilla. In all, twenty-one ships spent about a week in the bay and, as was the usual practice, crews spent some time ashore.

The boys sailing their own 'warships' of feathers and bits of driftwood are playing at a spot greatly favoured by Kirkwall children, near Cromwell Fort at the Mount. It is evident that the small lad at the back had been well warned, before leaving home, of the dangers of the deep and the penalties for getting soaked. Previous episodes would have told him that such warnings were not to be treated lightly.

PHOTOGRAPH BY TOM KENT, 1906

This spectacular display took place in May 1911, during the visit to Kirkwall of the 1st Destroyer Flotilla. It included HMS *Blenheim*, HMS *Amazon*, HMS *Tartar*, HMS *Swift* and the cruiser HMS *Blanche*, with Prince George, son of Prince Louis of Battenberg, on board as a midshipman. This visit was followed by exercises in the North Sea and a further two weeks in Orkney at Scapa Flow.

PHOTOGRAPH BY TOM KENT, 1911

One of the more significant events associated with Scapa Flow took place in the autumn of 1918, heralding the end of naval hostilities in the First World War. On the morning of Saturday 23 November the first of the newly captured German High Seas Fleet sailed, under escort, in through the Hoxa Sound boom to be interned indefinitely. Within one week a total of seventy-four German warships lay helplessly at anchor, with a skeleton crew of 1,800 men, where they were to remain until an even more spectacular event was to take place on 21 June 1919. Then, at noon, under the secret orders of Rear-Admiral Ludwig von Reuter, and before the startled eyes of its captives, this vast assembly of naval might opened its seacocks and disappeared slowly below the surface of Scapa Flow. This final act of defiance, the greatest scuttle of all time, was to initiate a new era of activity in the 'Flow', the greatest marine salvage operation of all time, which was to continue throughout the interwar years and resume operations after 1945. This view over Houton Seaplane Station gives some indication of the scale of what happened that fateful day.

PHOTOGRAPH BY TOM KENT, 1918

Among the many German warships that lay at the bottom of Scapa Flow was the *Hindenburg*, a battle-cruiser of 28,000 tons, which came to rest in 11½ fathoms of water. This great ship, built at Wilhelmshaven, was launched with much ceremony in 1915, the latest in German naval architecture. With a 700-foot waterline and a 96-foot beam, she was protected by 4-inch steel decking and a hull constructed of steel plating, 12 inches at the centre and tapering to 4 inches at each end. Her 63,000 horsepower turbines gave her a capability of 26½ knots, and she sported eight 12-inch guns, and fourteen 5.9-inch guns as her main armament.

In 1924 the first serious efforts in this massive salvage undertaking were begun by the firm of Cox & Danks, under the personal supervision of Ernest F.C. Cox. A number of smaller ships were raised and removed for scrap. Then, after several unsuccessful attempts between 1926 and 1930, he brought up the biggest prize of all, the *Hindenburg*, rich in metals and alloys, and had her towed to Rosyth on the Scottish mainland for breaking up. The system he employed was one he had perfected on other smaller ships in the group. All holes were sealed with heavy timber, metal, quick-drying concrete or cement and tallow, the water was then pumped out and she floated to the surface on her own, steadied by two large floating docks. The largest patch required on the *Hindenburg* measured 40 feet by 20 feet and weighed 11 tons. In all, Cox raised twenty-six destroyers, four battle-cruisers, two battleships and one light cruiser. When he decided to pull out, the operations were continued by Metal Industries, until what remained was considered to be uneconomical for salvage. Still lying on the sea bed are three battleships, the *König,* the *Markgraf* and the *Kronprinz Wilhelm*, and four light cruisers, the *Karlsruhe,* the *Brummer,* the *Dresden* and the *Köln*. Their existence has proved to be something of a tourist attraction, many subaqua divers coming from all over the world to explore their dark secrets.

PHOTOGRAPH BY WILLIAM HOURSTON, 1930

Diving has always been a hazardous occupation and for divers employed in the salvage of the German High Seas Fleet at Scapa Flow it was particularly dangerous. Working at depth, in the dark, often inside the hulls of large ships where trapped gases, debris, sharp edges that could damage diving suits or air feeds were all around; totally dependent on a team of men on the surface to keep their air supply constant and to react immediately to their every signal; and always at risk from the dreaded 'bends': death was never far away from these men. Much of the work involved new untried techniques, diving equipment was fairly primitive and risks were correspondingly high. As many as sixteen divers, each with his own support squad, worked on the *Hindenburg*. One of them, complete with copper helmet, waterproof suit with airline attached and surrounded by the apparent chaos of ropes, catwalks, pipes and seaweed, is all set for a day's work below the murky waters of the 'Flow'.

PHOTOGRAPH BY WILLIAM HOURSTON, *c.* 1925

Some of the many souvenirs brought out from one of the salvaged ships of the German High Seas Fleet, which was scuttled at Scapa Flow in 1919. They are still to be found in many households in Orkney as well as on exhibition in the Stromness Museum.

PHOTOGRAPH BY WILLIAM HOURSTON, *c.* 1925

During the First World War, many old merchant ships were commandeered and sunk in various entrances at Kirk or Holm Sound, Skerry Sound, East Weddel Sound and Water Sound, in order to protect the naval anchorage at Scapa Flow. In 1914 nineteen 'blockships' were placed and they seem to have served their purpose but when hostilities ended in 1918 their existence proved to be a nuisance to local shipping, particularly small fishing boats. Things came to a head when one small boat was smashed against one of the wrecks and lives were lost. The wrangle between the local authorities and the admiralty, as to whose responsibility they were, continued from 1920 to 1931 and, in fact, during this time only one ship, the *Aorangi*, was raised and towed away. Several other attempts failed miserably, something which

caused much local comment, since only a few miles away great battleships from the German High Seas Fleet were being raised by the firm of Cox & Danks, at regular intervals and with what appeared to be comparative ease. It indicated a distinct lack of enthusiasm in high places. By 1939 no further progress had been made and, of course, the whole picture had changed as once again we were at war with Germany. A further 70,000 tons of shipping were sunk to make the channels even more secure but on 14 October 1939 disaster struck in the form of a German submarine, the *U 47*, under the command of Gunther Prien. It entered the 'Flow' through the 'blocked' channel at Kirk Sound and torpedoed the battleship HMS *Royal Oak* at her moorings, with the loss of 800 men. This event finally

spurred the British Government into action and after personally inspecting the defences at Scapa, Winston Churchill ordered causeways to be built across the four entrances. The Churchill Barriers, as they came to be known, were constructed by Italian prisoners of war under the control of the firm Balfour and Beattie. A few of the old 'blockships' can still be seen rusting away along the causeways, which have become a valuable land link between the southern islands and the mainland of Orkney. This photograph shows 'blockships' in Kirk Sound during early salvage attempts, complete with walkways from ship to shore.

PHOTOGRAPH BY TOM KENT, *c.* 1920

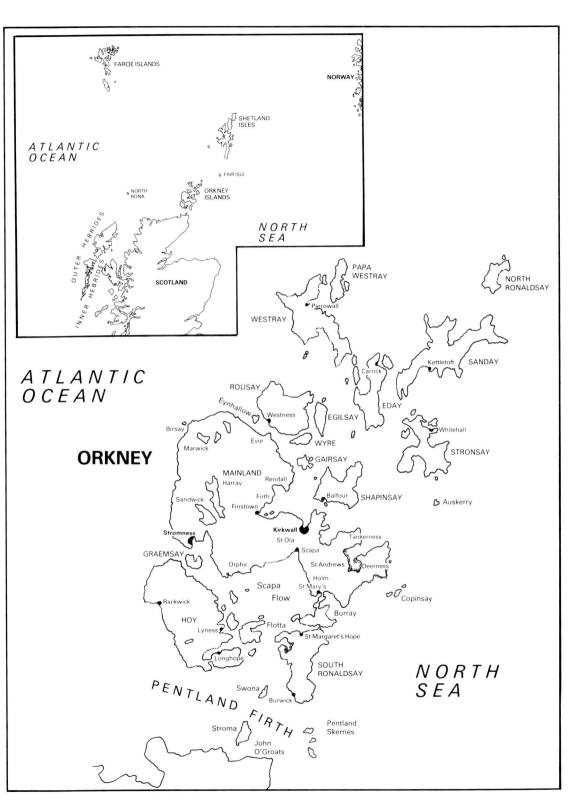

ATLANTIC
OCEAN

FAROE ISLANDS

NORWAY

SHETLAND
ISLES

FAIR ISLE

NORTH
RONA

ORKNEY
ISLANDS

OUTER HEBRIDES

INNER HEBRIDES

SCOTLAND

NORTH
SEA

ATLANTIC
OCEAN

ORKNEY

PAPA
WESTRAY

NORTH
RONALDSAY

Pierowall

WESTRAY

Kettletoft

SANDAY

Carrick

ROUSAY

Eynhallow

Westness

EGILSAY

EDAY

Whitehall

Birsay

Evie

WYRE

STRONSAY

Marwick

GAIRSAY

MAINLAND

Harray

Rendall

Sandwick

Firth

Balfour

SHAPINSAY

Auskerry

Finstown

Stromness

Kirkwall

Tankerness

St Ola

Scapa

GRAEMSAY

Orphir

St Andrews

Deerness

Holm

Scapa
Flow

St Mary's

Copinsay

Rackwick

Burray

HOY

Lyness

Flotta

St Margaret's Hope

Longhope

SOUTH
RONALDSAY

NORTH
SEA

Swona

Burwick

PENTLAND FIRTH

Stroma

Pentland
Skerries

John
O'Groats

Orkney today has a thriving population of around 19,500, scattered throughout eighteen of its seventy islands but concentrated chiefly in the two main-island towns of Kirkwall (6,700) and Stromness (2,000). The economic base is still agriculture although the impact of oil and the expansion of the fishing and tourist industries have enhanced the financial security of the community. The islands now are much more readily accessible than in the days depicted in this book, with daily air flights and sea ferries from Scotland, as well as regular inter-island services.

It is not the Orkney our forefathers knew but in spite of our 'progress' into the modern world of fast cars, fast food and above all, the fast buck, it is still truly possible to experience a quality of life that has little in common with current values. To hear, as they did, the haunting cry of the whaup, to smell wild mint on a dewy morning and to feel, with gentle hands, the leveret's anxious heartbeat – simple things that touched their senses and diverted them from the toils of everyday existence. Perhaps there is something for us to learn from these echoes of a time now gone.

NOTES ON THE PHOTOGRAPHERS

DAVID HORNE was born in 1877 in Kirkwall, where he trained under his father as a bacon curer, eventually taking over the family business in Mounthoolie Lane. He was a man of talents, producing several books of prose and poetry and he had a love and interest in his native islands that is well reflected in both pen and picture. As a photographer he was purely an amateur but he worked with good-quality equipment and, in time, he developed his skills to a degree that many a professional would have been proud of. Most of the wealth of material he produced was carefully preserved and thanks to the generosity of his daughter-in-law Margaret Horne, it is now part of our archive collection. He died in 1940.

WILLIAM HOURSTON was a more recent professional photographer who worked mainly in the Stromness area. Born in the main-island parish of Evie in 1895, he moved to Stromness in the 1930s where, for a time, he ran a billiard saloon and barber shop. His true interest, however, was in photography and the opportunity to express it came with the raising of the scuttled German High Seas Fleet in Scapa Flow. His recording of this, the greatest marine salvage operation ever tackled, is the most important feature of his collection. He also had a good eye for the picturesque and took many attractive views of Stromness – the most scenic corner of our island group. He continued to take pictures late into the 1950s, when he retired, and he remained in the town until his death in 1968.

TOM KENT was a professional photographer in Orkney from 1898 to 1936 and it is his work that is by far the most important contribution to our photographic archive. Born in the parish of Firth in 1863, he may well have been influenced by William Hugh Wood, who had been working as a semi-professional photographer in Finstown from about the time Kent was born. However, it was in Chicago, while working for a time in a drugstore, that young Tom learned his craft. When he returned to Orkney he set up shop as a professional, selling photographic equipment, stationery, fancy goods and books. More than just a recorder of events, he took great pains to take not just any picture but the best that he could. He had an artist's eye for composition and balance, as well as an acute awareness of what was important in the everyday things that surrounded him. The quality of his work was recognised outside Orkney and he contributed regularly to professional magazines, as well as having several articles included in *Country Life*. He used the most sophisticated equipment available at the time, some of which is in our local museum, and he experimented a great deal with new techniques. Success did not treat him kindly, however, and at the time of his death in 1936, he appears to have been largely shunned by the society that he so faithfully and brilliantly recorded.

ROBERT HEDDLE ROBERTSON was born on the island of South Ronaldsay in 1872 but moved to Stromness as a young man where he opened two grocery shops. He prospered well at a time when the herring fishing boom was at its peak. Though he did sell photographic equipment, as well as prints and postcards produced by himself, his interest in the craft developed more or less on an amateur basis but even if he did not reach the technical excellence of either Kent or Wood his work was good and contains much that was not recorded elsewhere. Though only in Stromness for fourteen years, he produced a great deal of material during that time, reflecting life as he saw it, mainly in the town and its immediate surroundings. By 1912 the herring industry had moved to the island of Stronsay and he decided to leave Stromness to take up an appointment as manager of the co-operative store on the island of Westray, where he continued to take photographs for many years, living to the grand old age of ninety. He died in 1962.

GEORGE WASHINGTON WILSON was not an Orcadian but he visited Orkney on two occasions, once in the 1880s and again in the 1890s, taking many pictures. He was born in 1823 in Culvie, Banffshire, and became a professional photographer of great renown, reputed to be the leading portrait photographer in Aberdeen during the 1850s, selected by Prince Albert to act as photographer to the royal family when they were in Scotland and considered to be the most prolific publisher of landscapes in Britain. His work cannot be ignored in any worthwhile collection of early photographs. Though we possess none of his negatives we are fortunate in having many of his prints depicting Orkney, from which we have been able to reproduce illustrations for this book. They are of immense value since they are among the earliest photographic records of life in the islands and of a quality that cannot be surpassed. He died in 1893.

WILLIAM HUGH WOOD was one of the first photographers practising in Orkney, certainly producing work by the 1870s and probably much earlier. He was born in 1830 in the main-island parish of Rendall but spent most of his life in the village of Finstown in the neighbouring parish of Firth, working as a postmaster but also taking pictures on a commercial basis. Portraiture was his special interest and his pictures are of obvious costume and genealogical appeal. The equipment and techniques he would have used were primitive by present-day standards but the results he produced were exceptional. We are fortunate to possess some of his original negatives and a number of prints. He died in 1903.

SELECT METRIC CONVERSIONS

1 cran	=	170.48 litres
1 cubic yard	=	0.76 cubic metre
1 fathom	=	1.83 metres
1 foot	=	0.30 metre
1 gallon	=	4.55 litres
1 hundredweight	=	50.80 kilograms
1 inch	=	2.54 centimetres
1 mile	=	1.61 kilometres
1 stone	=	6.35 kilograms
1 ton	=	1016.05 kilograms

12d. = 1 shilling = 5p